BEST EVER

101

Lawyer

Jokes

Matthew Burgess

Illustrations: Dyan Burgess

National Library of Australia Cataloguing-in-Publication entry

Creator:	Burgess, Matthew, author.
Title:	101 Lawyer Jokes / Matthew Burgess ; illustrator, Dyan Burgess.
ISBN:	978-1-925181-98-2 (createspace) 978-1-925181-99-9 (Kindle) 978-1-925181-31-9 (Smashwords)
Subjects:	Lawyers--Humor. Law--Humor. Practice of law--Humor.
Other Creators/Contributors:	Burgess, Dyan illustrator.
Dewey Number:	808.87

Published by D & M Fancy Pastry Pty Ltd
101 Lawyer Jokes
Copyright 2015 Matthew Burgess

Important disclaimer

The information in this book is of a general nature and is intended to be (at least for some) humorous. It is not intended to be professional advice.

The book is a collection of jokes provided to the author over time and no offence is intended in relation to any aspect of the book.

The author also wishes to convey that this is a book of jokes. It should not be taken out of context and items mentioned should not be tried or actually done. This book is merely for entertainment purposes.

Contents

Best Ever - 101 Lawyer Jokes

Chapter 1

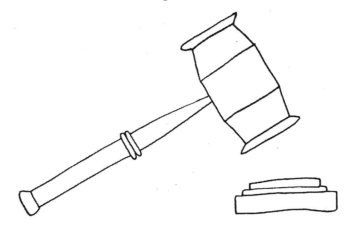

Court Room

The National Institute of Health (NIH) announced that they were going to start using lawyers instead of rats in their experiments. Naturally, the Lawyers Association was outraged and filed a court injunction. The NIH presented 4 main reasons for the switch, namely:

1. The lab assistants were becoming very attached to their little rats. This emotional involvement was interfering with the research being conducted. No such attachment could form for a lawyer.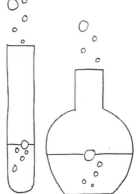

2. Lawyers breed faster and are in much greater supply.

3. Lawyers are much cheaper to care for and the humanitarian societies won't jump all over you, no matter what you're studying.

4. There are some things even a rat won't do.

Defendant: Judge, I want you to appoint me another lawyer.

Judge: And why is that?

Defendant: Because the Public Defender isn't interested in my case.

Judge (to Public Defender): Do you have any comments on the defendant's motion?

Public Defender: I'm sorry, your Honour. I wasn't listening.

JUST IN CASE YOU EVER GET THE TWO MIXED UP

IN PRISON you spend the majority of your time in an 8X10 cell;

AT WORK IN A LAW FIRM you spend the majority of your time in a 6X8 cubicle.

IN PRISON you get three meals a day;

AT WORK IN A LAW FIRM you only get a break for one meal and you have to pay for it.

IN PRISON you get time off for good behaviour;

AT WORK IN A LAW FIRM you get rewarded for good behaviour with more work.

IN PRISON the guard locks and unlocks all the doors for you;

AT WORK IN A LAW FIRM you must carry around a security card and open all the doors for yourself.

IN PRISON you can watch TV and play games;

AT WORK IN A LAW FIRM you get fired for watching TV and playing games.

IN PRISON you spend your time, as you deem appropriate to get tasks done effectively;

AT WORK IN A LAW FIRM you spend your time in the way the firm deems will create the maximum amount of chargeable hours.

IN PRISON you get your own toilet;

AT WORK IN A LAW FIRM you have to share.

IN PRISON they allow your family and friends to visit;

AT WORK IN A LAW FIRM you can't even speak to your family.

IN PRISON the taxpayers pay all expenses with no work required;

AT WORK IN A LAW FIRM you get to pay all the expenses to go to work and then they deduct taxes from your salary to pay for prisoners.

IN PRISON you spend most of your life looking through bars from inside wanting to get out;

AT WORK IN A LAW FIRM you spend most of your time wanting to get out and go inside bars.

IN PRISON there are wardens who are sadistic;

AT WORK IN A LAW FIRM they are called partners.

Actual Transcripts from the wonderful world of the Law Courts:

Q: What is your birth date?

A: July 15th.

Q: What year?

A: Every year.

Q: What gear were you in at the moment of the impact?

A: Gucci sweats and Reeboks.

Q: This myasthenia gravis - does it affect your memory at all?

A: Yes.

Q: And in what ways does it affect your memory?

A: I forget.

Q: You forget. Can you give us an example of something that you've forgotten?

Q: How old is your son - the one living with you.

A: Thirty-eight or thirty-five, I can't remember which.

Q: How long has he lived with you?

A: Forty-five years.

Q: And where was the location of the accident?

A: Approximately milepost 499.

Q: And where is milepost 499?

A: Probably between milepost 498 and 500.

The following are questions actually asked of witnesses by attorneys during trials and, in certain cases, the responses given by insightful witnesses:

Q: Now doctor, isn't it true that when a person dies in his sleep, he doesn't know about it until the next morning?

Q: The youngest son, the twenty-year old, how old is he?

_____

Q: Were you present when your picture was taken?

_____

Q: Was it you or your younger brother who was killed in the war?

_____

Q: Did he kill you?

_____

Q: How far apart were the vehicles at the time of the collision?

_____

Q: You were there until the time you left, is that true?

_____

Q: How many times have you committed suicide?

_____

Q: So the date of conception (of the baby) was August 8th?

A: Yes.

Q: And what were you doing at that time?

Q: She had three children, right?

A: Yes.

Q: How many were boys?

A: None.

Q: Were there any girls?

Q: You say the stairs went down to the basement?

A: Yes.

Q: And these stairs, did they go up also?

Q: How was your first marriage terminated?

A: By death.

Q: And by whose death was it terminated?

Q: Is your appearance here this morning pursuant to a deposition notice, which I sent to your attorney?

A: No, this is how I dress when I go to work.

Q: Doctor, how many autopsies have you performed on dead people?

A: All my autopsies are performed on dead people.

Q: All your responses must be oral, OK? Firstly, what school did you go to?

A: Oral.

Q: Do you recall the time that you examined the body?

A: The autopsy started around 8:30 p.m.

Q: And Mr Dennington was dead at the time?

A: No, he was sitting on the table wondering why I was doing an autopsy.

Q: Are you qualified to give a urine sample?

Fill to this line

SPECIMAN

Q: Doctor, before you performed the autopsy, did you check for a pulse?

A: No.

Q: Did you check for blood pressure?

A: No.

Q: Did you check for breathing?

A: No.

Q: So, then it is possible that the patient was alive when you began the autopsy?

A: No.

Q: How can you be so sure, Doctor?

A: Because his brain was sitting on my desk in a jar.

Q: But could the patient have still been alive nevertheless?

A: It is possible that he could have been alive and practicing law somewhere.

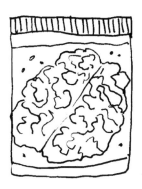

AND THE WINNER IS -

Q: Do you know if your daughter has ever been involved in the voodoo or occult?

A: We both do.

Q: Voodoo?

A: We do.

Q: You do?

A: Yes, voodoo.

A defence attorney was cross-examining a police officer during a felony trial – it went like this:

Q. Officer, did you see my client fleeing the scene?

A. No sir, but I subsequently observed a person matching the description of the offender running several blocks away.

Q. Officer, who provided this description?

A. The officer who responded to the scene.

Q. A fellow officer provided the description of this so-called offender. Do you trust your fellow officers?

A. Yes, sir, with my life.

Q. With your life? Let me ask you this, then, officer-do you have a locker room in the police station - a room where you change your clothes in preparation for your daily duties?

A. Yes sir, we do.

Q. And do you have a locker in that room?

A. Yes sir, I do.

Q. And do you have a lock on your locker?

A. Yes sir.

Q. Now why is it, officer, if you trust your fellow officers with your life, that you find it necessary to lock your locker in a room?

A. Sometimes lawyers have been known to walk through that room.

With that, the courtroom erupted in laughter, and a prompt recess was called. The officer on the stand has been nominated for this year's best comeback line.

A lawyer, testifying in a case about his performance, is asked, "How good are you at what you do?"

His response: "I am the greatest lawyer in the world."

The judge said, "There is no need to be boastful, indeed, some modesty would probably help your cause."

The lawyer responded, "Thank you, your Honour, however I am under oath."

Dictation Guidelines for Lawyers dictating court related matters

Adherence to these guidelines will assure the highest quality transcribed letters in the shortest amount of time.

At the beginning of the dictation, take as deep a breath as you possibly can. Now, try to dictate the entire tape before you have to inhale again.

When dictating a particularly difficult word or phrase, please turn your head and speak directly into your armpit.

We charge per character, including periods. An effective way to cut your cost is to dictate your entire letter as one sentence.

It is not necessary to repeat the same sentence multiple times in the same dictation.

If you have to sneeze or cough suddenly, please remove your head from your armpit and sneeze or cough directly into the microphone.

If you must eat while you dictate, please stay away from foods such as marshmallows, bananas, and pudding. Apples, pretzels, and celery are much better choices.

Please do not stop dictating when you yawn, it throws off our rhythm.

If the client's name is Alan Ratzlaffenhasenphepherzinsky, please have the courtesy to spell "Alan- - there are several possible spellings, you know. For the last name, simply state "the usual spelling".

Do not stop dictating in the event of minor background noise such as an office party, the janitor's vacuum cleaner, a screaming infant, etc. Again, it throws off our rhythm.

Be sure to place the emphasis on the correct syllable, especially if English is your second language.

Talk as fast as you can. Fair is fair; after all we type as fast as we can.

It is not necessary to repeat the same sentence multiple times in the same dictation.

Please speak as quietly as you can, we want to be able to hear what's going on around you.

If you need to pause for 5 or 10 minutes between words or phrases, pounding the receiver on the desk or repeatedly saying, "still dictating ... still dictating ... still dictating ... still dictating..." reminds us that indeed, you are still dictating.

Just because you need to use the restroom is no reason to stop dictating. Time is money.

Do not dictate so loudly that you disrupt your fellow lawyers' football game in the staff kitchen. In fact, you really should whisper all of your dictation since the information is confidential.

Similarly if you are going to watch TV while dictating at

home, please watch a war movie with lots of bombing, and be sure to have the volume high enough so everybody in your living room can hear above your talking.

If you need to correct yourself - sorry, correct an error,

please do not rewind the tape - sorry, do not back up- and record over the error - sorry, wait, the mistake - just continue with the sentence - wait - go back with the paragraph and fix the error - err, the mistake.

Please go back and just delete that last guideline.

When dictating on your mobile phone from your car, be sure to go through as many tunnels as possible. This will help ensure confidentiality of the information.

Finally you (y -o-u), do not need (n-e-e-d) to spell (s-p-e-l-l) obvious words (w-o-r-d-s) for us (u-s). It is our job (j-o--b) to know (k-n-o-w) how to (t-o) spell words that (t-h-a-t) we learned (l-e-a-r-n-e-d) in third (t-h-i-r-d) grade (g-r-a-d-e).

Excerpts from a recent NZ High Court decision:

"What is the modern world coming to when a gang of thieves arrives at the place they are going to rob in a taxi?" Justice Morris asked the defendants in a robbery case at the Auckland High Court. "I despair of the future for our country when a group of louts like you lack the intelligence to take even basic precautions to avoid detection."

Before sentencing Singeli Senivuga and Veileba Jobesa (two illegal Fijian immigrants) for their part in the robbery of 5 protective helmets and 400 puncture repair kits from an Mt Eden bicycle shop, Justice Morris continued: "It has been put to me that the reason you were so easily apprehended after the robbery was that you had no getaway car. According to your defence counsel, that is because you forgot to ask the taxi to wait for you while you committed the crime.

"But even more stupidly, you had telephoned the taxi service in the first place and asked to be picked up at your home, so even if you had gotten away, it would have been a simple matter to locate and arrest you later."

The judge then added: "Why couldn't you steal a car beforehand, like everybody else? You tell me it's because you don't have licences, but I preside daily over cases involving professional criminals who don't care about such trivial matters. You are imbeciles. I hereby sentence you both to five years imprisonment."

Actual label instructions on consumer goods approved by lawyers and the court system

On a blanket from Taiwan:

NOT TO BE USED AS PROTECTION FROM A TORNADO

On a helmet-mounted mirror used by US cyclists:

REMEMBER. OBJECTS IN THE MIRROR ARE ACTUALLY BEHIND YOU

On a Korean kitchen knife:

KEEP OUT OF CHILDREN

On an Indonesian packet of nuts:

OPEN PACKET AND EAT CONTENTS

On a pack of Sainsbury's (UK) salted peanuts:

WARNING: CONTAINS NUTS

On a Taiwanese shampoo:

USE REPEATEDLY FOR SEVERE DAMAGE

On a Marks and Spencer's (UK) bread and butter pudding:

WARNING: PRODUCT WILL BE HOT AFTER HEATING

On the bottle-top of a flavoured milk drink:

AFTER OPENING. KEEP UPRIGHT

On an Aussie iron:

WARNING: NEVER IRON CLOTHES ON THE BODY.

On a New Zealand insect spray:

THIS PRODUCT NOT TESTED ON ANIMALS.

In an American guide to setting up a new computer:

TO AVOID CONDENSATION FORMING. ALLOW THE BOXES TO WARM UP TO ROOM TEMPERATURE BEFORE OPENING. (Sensible, but the instruction was on the INSIDE of the box.)

On a Japanese product used to relieve painful haemorrhoids:

LIE DOWN ON BED AND INSERT POSCOOL SLOWLY UP TO THE PROJECTED PORTION LIKE A SWORD-GUARD INTO ANAL DUCT WHILE INSERTING POSCOOL FOR APPROXIMATELY 5 MINUTES. KEEP QUIET.

On some Swann frozen dinners:

SERVING SUGGESTION - DEFROST.

On Sears's hair dryer:

DO NOT USE WHILE SLEEPING.

On a bag of Fritos:

YOU COULD BE A WINNER! NO PURCHASE NECESSARY. DETAILS INSIDE.

On a bar of Dial soap:

DIRECTIONS: USE LIKE REGULAR SOAP.

On a hotel provided shower cap in a box:

FITS ONE HEAD.

On a string of Chinese-made Christmas lights:

FOR INDOOR OR OUTDOOR USE ONLY.

On Tesco's tiramisu dessert:

DO NOT TURN UPSIDE DOWN. (Printed on bottom of the box)

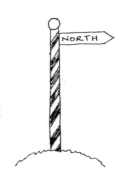

On Boot's children's cough medicine:

DO NOT DRIVE CAR OR OPERATE MACHINERY.

On Nytol sleep aid:

WARNING: MAY CAUSE DROWSINESS.

On a Japanese food processor:

NOT TO BE USED FOR THE OTHER USE.

On a child's Superman costume:

WEARING OF THIS GARMENT DOES NOT ENABLE YOU TO FLY.

On a Swedish chainsaw:

DO NOT ATTEMPT TO STOP CHAIN WITH YOUR HANDS OR GENITALS.

Chapter 2

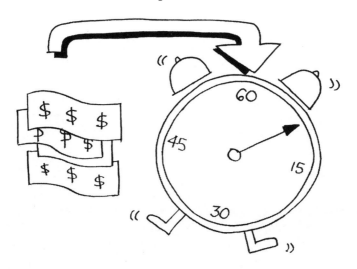

The Billable Hour

What's the difference between a good lawyer and a bad lawyer? A bad lawyer can let a case drag out for several years. A good lawyer can make it last even longer.

A lawyer dies and goes to Heaven.

"There must be some mistake," the lawyer argues. "I'm too young to die. I'm only 55."

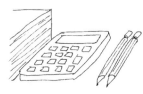

"Fifty-five?" says Saint Peter. "No, according to our calculations, you're 82."

"How'd you get that?" the lawyer asks.

St. Peter answers, "We added up your time sheets."

The lawyer's son wanted to follow in his father's footsteps, so he went to law school and graduated with honours. Then he went home to join his father's firm.

At the end of his first day at work, he rushed into his father's office and said, "Father, Father! In one day I broke the Smith case that you've been working on for so long!"

His father yelled, "You idiot! We've been living on the funding of that case for ten years!"

LAWYER SELF-IMPROVEMENT

They've got to be kidding, those lurid self-improvement manuals screaming at us from their own special section of every bookshop whenever you go in for a quiet browse.

As a lawyer whose entire worth depends on how many hours they can charge for every single task, there is a significant downside to improving, other than superficially, in anything work-related. Improving in a personal sense creates a dangerous precedent that should be actively avoided, lest it cause a flow-on impact on your legal career.

In any event, all the self-help books say the same thing. Some things are good for your legal career (e.g. get up earlier so you can work longer, work out in the gym so you can work longer); however some are dangerous beyond words (e.g. plan in detail before starting anything, so you can do things better, and exercise ruthless willpower in a relentless pursuit of effective objectives and efficient systems).

I find this sort of one-sided approach totally intimidating and suspect a capitalist plot by a consortium of clients and their overpaid chief executive officers to wring even more out of their underpaid lawyers.

Lawyers must understand what parts of the self-help books actually will help them and those that don't.

Here is the alternative for us lawyers, a methodology guaranteed to bring success.

THE 10 PRINCIPLES OF SUCCESS IN THE LAW

1. NEVER PLAN: Planning is a boring, unproductive activity and reduces the total number of chargeable hours available. Scientists have proved that life is too chaotic to plan anything successfully. Trying to make an effective plan is 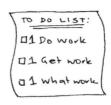 discouraging and unnecessarily risks saving otherwise fully chargeable time. You may never do what you set out to do if you go down this road, the task will seem not expensive enough and you'll give up in despair.

2. DREAM: Dreams are far nicer than plans. They can be enjoyed while you stay in bed long after all the planners have gone off to work. Just let fancies drift deliciously into your mind. Be excited by them but don't try to refine – all you should focus on is capturing all these thoughts on your time sheet, as they are clearly chargeable. Let the muddling process take care of the details later. And don't feel guilty - you've started work.

3. WARM TO THE TASK: Take a nice long shower where  you can crystallise your chargeable dreams enough to contemplate starting further chargeable work for the client. If possible, dream about more than one client at once so you can achieve 'double timing' entries on your time sheet. Take your time over this because once that glass door shuts behind you, it's a world of confusion and delusion out there. I suspect that under the shower is the only place to think constructively, not at the drawing board or staring at a blank computer screen at six in the morning. Enjoy a leisurely breakfast and maybe have a short stroll (none of this power walking). Now you are in the right frame of mind to start, as long as you have captured all the further chargeable thinking on your time sheet (note: there are now apps available to capture all the time entries on your smart phone).

4. BEGIN: Go mindlessly to where you intend to work - at the computer, in the workshop, or the garden. The crucial moment has arrived and so we want to take as much time as possible. Muddling is not to be confused with indecision. So - just start. Don't think about where; just do the first thing that comes into your head.

5. RESTART: After a few minutes (or hopefully, a few fully chargeable hours), it will become clear that you are on the wrong track and you will see where the start should really have been made. This is positive. You can now start all over again, this time in the realisation that you have muddled onto the right track and charges every minute to get there. Note, however, before you start again, ensure that all time spent is fully recorded on your time sheet. The process has started working for you. The bit done before will probably come in useful later anyway and is fully chargeable.

6. TRIAL AND ERROR: This is the core of the process. Proceed in any haphazard way that suits and ensure all time spent is captured on your time sheet. Don't be frightened of going wrong - nothing is wrong without the straitjacket of a plan. Having no preconceived plan gives you the flexibility to go blissfully down any new path. Also feel free, once you have provided the charge code, to speak to as many other lawyers in the firm about any aspect of the job that might have any potential insights. Indeed having meetings with no agendas with multiple lawyers is a fantastic way to help everyone meet their billable hours or targets.

7. PACE YOURSELF: The secret is a little at a time, frequently. Feel like a break? Take it. Many of these breaks can be fully chargeable as long as you are thinking  or dreaming broadly about a client's situation. Six hours a day of actual work is enough for anyone; working longer is unproductive. This is key to exceeding chargeable targets. You'll get lots more billable units if you do actual work for around 6 hours while ensuring you have enough chargeable breaks and interruptions to be at work for at least 12 hours. Once you have put a work task aside, though, do not come back to it for at least a day as that will allow you

to go back to step 5 (i.e. RESTART). This said, you could have an afternoon nap, and dream further chargeable dreams about clients. Just remember to fill in your time sheet when you wake up until the smart phone app that allows your dreams to be automatically converted into time sheet entries is released.

8. LIVE WITH CLUTTER: If your desk or workbench gets untidy while you are at work, don't worry, just keep going. Lawyers who are able to cope with confusion possess superior intelligence by accessing the chargeable 'Research' code (i.e. you can re-search your room for the work you have lost). When it's time to do something else for a change, this is the time to sweep up or tidy the desktop. If you really feel like it. Again, this task is effectively 'Research' as well so all client work tidied away should be charged.

9. THE WAY AHEAD: As the task muddles along, there will come a time when a shape emerges, the way becomes clear in a far more detailed and integrated way than could ever have been planned for. Normally this is about the time when you realise (or your partner reminds you) that the file cannot be milked any further, so it needs to be closed. Go for it, just ensure you charge all time.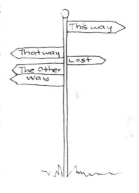

10. THE LAST STEP: I can't think of one. I should never have planned for 10. See what I mean? That'll have to do. This said, the time thinking about an idea for a client that results in nothing is clearly chargeable – time billing is all about the inputs, outputs are irrelevant to your budget so ignore them whenever possible.

A doctor gets a phone call from his lawyer, and the frantic voice at the other end says, "I am SO stressed I have shot and I think killed the junior lawyer working for me because they had not filled out their time sheet - what on earth do I do?"

The doctor tells his lawyer friend to calm down and says, "OK, now the first thing is, you have to be sure that he's really dead."

There is silence at the other end, then a single gunshot, before the lawyer asks, "OK, that did it. What next?"

You have just got to love lawyers driven to make the billable hour as profitable as possible.

Pythagoras' Theorem: ....24 words.
Lord's Prayer: ....66 words.
Archimedes' Principle: ....67 words.
Ten Commandments: ....179 words.
Gettysburg Address: ....286 words.
US Declaration of Independence: ....1,300 words.
US Constitution with all
27 Amendments: .... 7,818 words.
Legal Regulations on the Sale of
CABBAGES in the EU:......26,911 words

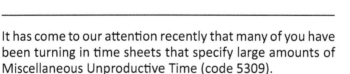

It has come to our attention recently that many of you have been turning in time sheets that specify large amounts of Miscellaneous Unproductive Time (code 5309).

To our firm, unproductive time is not a problem. What is a problem, however, is not knowing exactly what you are doing with your unproductive time. The newly installed Activity-Based Costing Financial system requires additional information to achieve its goals.

Attached below is a sheet specifying a tentative extended job code list based on our observations of employee activities. The list will allow you to specify with better precision what you are doing during your unproductive time. Please begin using this job code list immediately and let us know about any difficulties you may encounter.

Extended Task Code List

Code   Explanation:

5000   Surfing the Net

5001   Reading/Writing Social Email

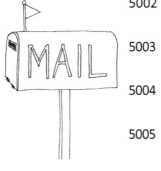

5002   Sharing Social E-Mail (see codes #5003, #5004)

5003   Collecting Jokes and Other Humorous Material via E-Mail

5004   Forwarding Jokes and Other Humorous Material via E-Mail

5005   Faxing Jokes and Other Humorous Material to Friends not on E-Mail

5316   Meeting

5317   Obstructing Communications at Meeting

5318   Trying to Sound Knowledgeable While in Meeting

5319   Waiting for Break

5320   Waiting for Lunch

5321   Waiting for End of Day

5322   Vicious Verbal Attacks Directed at Co-worker

5323   Vicious Verbal Attacks Directed at Co-worker while Co-worker Is not present

5393   Covering for Incompetence of Co-worker Friend

5400   Trying to Explain Concept to Co-worker Who Is Not Interested in Learning

5401   Trying to Explain Concept to Co-worker Who is Stupid

5402   Trying to Explain Concept to Co-worker Who Hates you on Principle

5403   Trying to Explain Concept to Co-worker Who Hates you because you wouldn't Sleep with them

5481   Buying Snack

5482   Eating Snack

5500   Filling out Time Sheet

5501   Inventing Time Sheet Entries

5502   Waiting for Something to Happen

5503   Scratching yourself

5504   Sleeping

5510   Feeling Bored

5600   Bitching about Lousy Job (see code #5610)

5601   Bitching about Low Pay (see code #5610)

5602   Bitching about Long Hours (see code #5610)

5603   Bitching about Co-worker (see codes #5322, #5323)

5604   Bitching about Boss (see code #5610)

5605   Bitching about Personal Problems

5610   Searching for a New Job

5640   Miscellaneous Unproductive Bitching

5701   Not Actually Present at Job

5702   Suffering from Eight-Hour Flu

6102   Ordering out

6103   Waiting for Food Delivery to Arrive

6104   Taking it Easy while Digesting Food

6200   Using Company Resources for Personal Profit

6201   Stealing Company Goods

6202   Making Excuses after Accidentally Destroying Company Goods

6203   Using Company Phone to Make Long-Distance Personal Calls

6206   Gossiping

6207   Planning a Social Event

6210   Feeling Sorry for yourself

6221   Pretending to Work While Boss is Watching

6222   Pretending to Enjoy My Job

6223   Pretending I Like My Co-workers

6224   Pretending I Like Important people When in Reality They Are Jerks

6238   Miscellaneous Unproductive Fantasizing

6601   Running your Own Business on Company Time (see code #6603)

6602   Complaining

6603   Writing a Book on Company Time

6604   Planning a vacation on Company Time

6611   Staring into Space

6612   Staring at Computer Screen

6615   Transcendental Meditation

7281   Extended Trip to the Bathroom (at least 10 min.)

7400   Talking with Divorce Lawyer on Phone

7401   Talking with Plumber on Phone

7402   Talking with Dentist on Phone

7403   Talking with Doctor on Phone

7404   Talking with Masseuse on Phone

7405   Talking with House Painter on Phone

7406   Talking with Personal Therapist on Phone

7419   Talking with Miscellaneous Paid Professional on Phone

7425   Talking with Mistress / Toy Boy on Phone (also see code #7400)

7931   Asking a Co-worker to Aid Me in an Illicit Activity

8000   Recreational Drug Use

Chapter 3

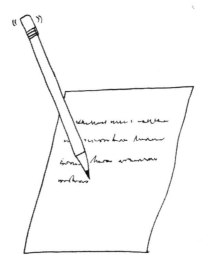

One-liners

99 percent of lawyers give the rest a bad name.

You never really learn to swear until you start dealing with a lawyer who charges by time.

For lawyers to succeed in politics, it is often necessary that they rise above their principles.

You have the right to remain silent. Anything you say will be misquoted then used against you.

My lawyer told me on the phone yesterday that they had just got lost in thought. Apparently it was unfamiliar territory for them.

There are two kinds of lawyers: those who know the law and those who know the judge.

Mark Twain notes...

"It is interesting to note that criminals have multiplied of late, and lawyers have also; but I repeat myself."

If a taxman and a lawyer were both drowning and you could only save one, would you go to lunch or read the paper?

I am a lawyer. I can only please one person per day. Today is not your day. Tomorrow is not looking good either.

Like all lawyers I love deadlines. I especially like the whooshing sound they make as they go flying by.

Never argue with an idiot lawyer. They drag you down to their level, and then beat you with experience.

Lawyer survival strategy - when you don't know what to do, walk fast and look worried.

Lawyer survival strategy - when confronted by a difficult problem, you can solve it more easily by reducing it to the question, "How would the Lone Ranger handle this?"

When you go into court, you are putting yourself in the hands of twelve people who weren't smart enough to get out of Jury duty.

Lawyer says client is not that guilty.

Why is it that lawyers call what they do "practice"?

And God said: "Let there be Satan, so people don't blame everything on me. And let there be lawyers, so people don't blame everything on Satan." - John Wing

Lawyer Mantras –

1. I wished the buck stopped here, as I could use a few.

2. Don't be irreplaceable. If you can't be replaced, you can't be promoted.

3. Always remember you're unique. Just like everyone else.

4. If you lend a client $20 and never see that person again, it was probably worth it.

5. Partners do not suffer from stress. They are a carrier.

6. Aim to record all time and work slower than a herd of turtles stampeding through peanut butter.

7. After any salary raise, you will have less money at the end of the month than you did before.

8. The more crap you put up with, the more crap you are going to get.

9. You can go anywhere you want if you look serious and carry a clipboard.

10. When you don't know what to do, walk fast and look worried.

11. No one is listening until you make a mistake.

Chapter 4

Q & A

Q: Santa Claus, the tooth fairy, an honest lawyer, and an old drunk are walking down the street together when they simultaneously spot a hundred dollar bill. Who gets it?

A: The old drunk, of course, the other three are fantasy creatures.

Q: What did the lawyer do to liven up the office party?

A: Not show up.

Q: What do you call 500 dead lawyers on the bottom of the ocean floor?

A: A good start.

Q: How many lawyer jokes are there?

A: Only one. The rest are true stories.

Q: What's wrong with lawyer jokes?

A: Lawyers don't think they're funny and other people don't think they're jokes.

Q: What do you call 25 skydiving lawyers?

A: Skeet.

Q: What do you call a lawyer gone bad?

A: Senator.

Q: What's the difference between a lawyer and an onion?

A: You cry when you cut up an onion.

Q: What do you call a lawyer with an IQ of 70?

A: Your honour.

Q: What do you throw to a drowning lawyer?

A: His partners.

Q: How can you tell when a lawyer is lying?

A: His lips are moving.

Q: What's the difference between a lawyer and a vulture?

A: The lawyer gets frequent flyer miles.

Q: If you have a bad lawyer, why not get a new one?

A: Changing lawyers is like moving to a different deck chair on the Titanic.

Q: How does an attorney sleep?

A: First he lies on one side and then on the other.

Q: What's the difference between a shame and a pity?

A: If a busload of lawyers goes over a cliff, and there are no survivors, that's known as a pity. If there were any empty seats, that's a shame.

Q: How do you get a group of lawyers to smile for a photo?

A: Just say, "Chargeable units!"

Q: How many lawyers does it take to change a light bulb?

A: Three. One to climb the ladder, one to shake it and one to sue the ladder company.

Q: Why do lawyers never go to the beach?

A: (No, it's not because there is not a billing code on their time sheet for it) Cats keep trying to bury them.

Q: What is black and brown and looks great on a lawyer?

A: A Doberman.

Q: Why do professional ethics prevent lawyers sleeping with their clients?

A: To prevent clients being billed twice for essentially the same service.

Q: What's the difference between a lawyer and a leech?

A: A leech drops off when you're dead.

Q: What do lawyers use for birth control?

A: Their personalities.

Q: If you see a lawyer on a bicycle, why should you never swerve to hit him?

A: It could be your bicycle.

Q: You're trapped in a room with a tiger, a snake, and a lawyer. You have a gun with two bullets. What do you do?

A: Shoot the lawyer - twice.

Q: What's the difference between a lawyer and a jet engine?

A: A jet engine eventually stops whining.

Q: What do you have when 100 lawyers are buried up to their neck in sand?

A: Not enough sand.

Q: What's the difference between a dead skunk in the road and a dead lawyer in the middle of the road?

A: There are skid marks in front of the skunk.

41

Q: Did you hear that the Post Office just recalled their latest stamp?

A: They had pictures of lawyers on them and people couldn't figure out which side to spit on.

Q: What is the lawyer's creed?

A: A client is innocent until proven broke.

Q: What's the difference between a female lawyer and a pit bull?

A: Lipstick.

Q: It was so cold last winter ... (How cold was it?)

A: I saw a lawyer with his hands in his own pocket.

Q: What happens when a male lawyer takes Viagra?

A: He gets taller.

Q: Why is it best to bury lawyers 6 feet underground following death?

A: Because deep down, they are actually nice people.

Q: What did the lawyer call the sushi bar she owned?

A: Just sue me.

Q: How many lawyers does it take to change a light bulb?

A: Whereas the party of the first part, also known as "Lawyer", and the party of the second part, also known as "Light Bulb", do hereby and forthwith agree to a transaction wherein the party of the second part (Light Bulb) shall be removed from the current position as a result of failure to perform previously agreed upon duties, i.e. e. the lighting, elucidation, and otherwise illumination of the area ranging from the front (north) door, through the entryway, terminating at an area just inside the primary living area, demarcated by the beginning of the carpet, any spill over illumination being at the option of the party of the second part (Light Bulb) and not required by the aforementioned agreement between the parties. The aforementioned removal transaction shall include, but not be limited to, the following steps:

1. The party of the first part (Lawyer) shall, with or without elevation at his option, by means of a chair, step stool, ladder or any other means of elevation, grasp the party of the second part (Light Bulb) and rotate the party of the second part (Light Bulb) in a counter-clockwise direction, this point being non-negotiable.

2. Upon reaching a point where the party of the second part (Light Bulb) becomes separated from the party of the third part ("Receptacle"), the party of the first part (Lawyer) shall have the option of disposing of the party of the second part (Light Bulb) in a manner consistent with all applicable state, local, and federal statutes.

3. Once separation and disposal have been achieved, the party of the first part (Lawyer) shall have the option of beginning installation of the party of the fourth part ("New Light Bulb").

This installation shall occur in a manner consistent with the reverse of the procedures described in step one of this self-same document, being careful to note that the rotation should occur in# a clockwise direction, this point also being non-negotiable.

#Note: The above described steps may be performed, at the option of the party of the first part (Lawyer), by any or all persons authorized by him, the objective being to produce the most possible revenue for the party of the fifth part, also known as Partnership.

Q: How do lawyers prefer to give season's greetings?

A: From me ("the wishor") to you ("hereinafter called the wishee")

Please accept without obligation, implied or implicit, my best wishes for an environmentally conscious, socially responsible, politically correct, low stress, non-addictive, gender neutral, celebration of the winter (or in acknowledgement of southern hemispheric seasonal inversion, summer) solstice holiday, practised within the most enjoyable traditions of the religious persuasion of your choice, or secular practices of your choice, with respect for the religious/secular persuasions and/or traditions of others, or their choice not to practice religious or secular traditions at all and a financially successful, personally fulfilling and medically 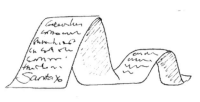 uncomplicated recognition of the onset of the generally accepted next chronological calendar year, but with due respect for the calendars of choice of other cultures or sects, and having regard to the race, creed, colour, age, physical ability, religious faith, choice of computer platform or dietary preference of the wishee.

By accepting this greeting you are bound by these terms that-

1. This greeting is subject to further clarification or withdrawal.

2. This greeting is freely transferable provided that no alteration shall be made to the original greeting and that the proprietary rights of the wishor are acknowledged.

3. This greeting implies no promise by the wishor to actually implement any of the wishes.

4. This greeting may not be enforceable in certain jurisdictions and/or the restrictions herein may not be binding upon certain wishees in certain jurisdictions and is revocable at the sole discretion of the wishor.

5. This greeting is warranted to perform as reasonably as may be expected within the usual application of good tidings, for a period of one year or until the issuance of a subsequent holiday greeting, whichever comes first.

6. The wishor warrants this greeting only for the limited replacement of this wish or issuance of a new wish at the sole discretion of the wishor.

7. Any references in this greeting to "the Lord", "Father Christmas", "Our Saviour", or any other festive figures, whether actual or fictitious, dead or alive, shall not imply any endorsement by or from them in respect of this greeting, and all proprietary rights in any referenced third party names and images are hereby acknowledged.

{IMPORTANT DISCLAIMER - without admission of liability, parts of this greeting may have been adapted from one or more existing precedents.}

Chapter 5

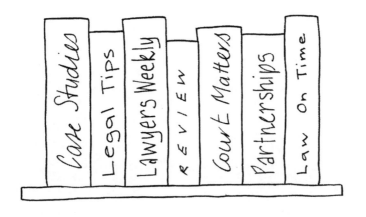

Story time

A girl asks her boyfriend to come over Friday night and have dinner with her parents for the first time so they could share their happy news that they were going to get married.

While, the guy is ecstatic, he wants to ensure he protects all of his assets so that she cannot access them if they bust up.

The guy meets his lawyer and explains all aspects of the relationship with his girlfriend, but that he suspects she is only interested in his money and that her parents would want to take him to the cleaners, particularly if any of them find out that he is sleeping with his girlfriend's sister as well.

After about 4 hours the guy and his lawyer build a series of complex trusts that the lawyer is certain will hide all assets from the vulture girlfriend, her sister and the parents when things inevitably sour.

That night the guy shows up at the girl's parents' house, and meets his girlfriend at the door. "Oh I'm so excited that you're finally meeting my parents, come on in!" she says.

The guy goes inside and is taken to the dinner table where the girl's parents are seated.

The guy quickly offers to say grace and bows his head.

A minute passes, and the guy is still deep in prayer, with his head down.

Ten minutes pass, and still no movement from the guy.

Finally, after 20 minutes with his head down the girlfriend leans over and whispers to the boyfriend, "I had no idea that you were this religious."

The boy turns and whispers back, "I had no idea that your father was a trust lawyer."

This happened to an Englishman in France who was totally drunk.

The French policeman stops his car and asks the gentleman if he has been drinking. With great difficulty, the Englishman admits that he has been drinking all day, that his daughter got married in the morning to a French man, and that he drank champagne and a few bottles of wine at the reception and a quite few glasses of single malt thereafter.

Quite upset, the policeman proceeds to alcotest (breath test) him and asks the Englishman if he knows under French Law why he is going to be arrested.

The Englishman answers with humour: "No, sir, I do not! But while we're asking questions, do you know that this is a British car and my wife is driving on the other side?"

A conversation overheard in the men's room: an accountant, a lawyer, and a cowboy were standing side-by-side using the urinal.

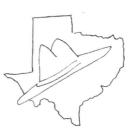

The accountant finished, zipped up and started washing and literally scrubbing his hands, clear up to his elbows. He used about 20 paper towels before he finished. He turned to the other two men and commented, "I graduated from the University of Michigan and they taught us to be clean."

The lawyer finished, zipped up, quickly wet the tips of his fingers, grabbed one paper towel and commented,

"I graduated from the University of California and they taught us to be environmentally conscious."

The cowboy finished, zipped up, and as he was walking out the door, said, "I graduated from Texas Tech University and they taught us not to wee on our hands!"

Once upon a time a boy was walking down the road when a car pulled over. "If you get in," the driver said, "I'll give you $10." The boy ignored the approach and kept on walking.

A bit further along, the man pulled over again. "Ok, how about $20 and a bag of lollies?" the driver asks.

The boy told the man to get lost, and kept on walking.

Further up the road, the driver tried once more.

"Right, this is my final offer, I'll give you $50 and all the lollies you can eat."

The boy finally snaps and says "Dad – you decided to be a lawyer, live with it!"

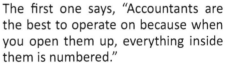

Four surgeons are taking a coffee break.

The first one says, "Accountants are the best to operate on because when you open them up, everything inside them is numbered."

The second surgeon says, "Nah, librarians are the best; everything inside them is in alphabetical order."

Third surgeon says, "Try electricians. Everything inside them is colour-coded."

The fourth one says, "I prefer lawyers. They're heartless, spineless, gutless and their heads and bums are interchangeable."

Once upon a time there was a shepherd tending his sheep at the edge of a country road. A brand new Jeep Grand Cherokee screeches to a halt next to him.

The driver, a young man dressed in a Brioni suit, Cerrutti shoes, Ray-Ban glasses, Jovial Swiss wrist watch and a BHS tie gets out and asks the shepherd: "If I guess how many sheep you have, will you give me one of them?"

The shepherd looks at the young man, then looks at the sprawling field of sheep and says: "Okay."

The young man parks the SUV, connects his notebook and wireless modem, and enters a NASA site, scans the ground using his GPS, opens a database and 60 Excel tables filled with algorithms, then prints a 150-page report on his high tech mini printer. He then asks three other team members to read the report from cover to cover and they have a long meeting to discuss its contents, before a fourth team member conducts a peer review, prior to a further meeting.

Finally, at every step of the process he, and each team member, fill in a timesheet listing all the things they did, rounding up each entry to the nearest hour. He then turns to the shepherd and says: "You have exactly 1,586 sheep here."

The shepherd answers: "That's correct, you can have your sheep."

The young man takes one of the animals and puts it in the back of his vehicle.

The shepherd looks at him and asks: "Now, if I guess your profession, will you pay me back in kind?"

The young man answers: "Sure."

The shepherd says: "You are a lawyer."

"Exactly! How did you know?" asks the young man.

"Very simple," answers the shepherd.

"First, you came here without being called.

"Second, you charged me a fee to tell me something I already knew, based on the number of hours you claim you spent.

"Third, you do not understand anything about my business and I'd really like to have my dog back."

In California, more than 600 lawyer hopefuls were taking the State Bar exams in the Pasadena Convention Centre when a 50-year-old man taking the test suffered a heart attack. Only two of the 600 test takers, Jim Leslie and Eunice Morgan, stopped to help the man. They administered CPR until paramedics arrived, then resumed taking the exam.

Citing policy, the test supervisor refused to allow the two additional time to make up for the 40 minutes they spent helping the victim. Jerome Braun, the State Bar's senior executive for admissions, backed the decision stating, "If these two want to be lawyers, they should learn a lesson about priorities."

A busload of lawyers was driving down a country road, when suddenly the bus ran off the road and crashed into an old farmer's barn.

The old farmer got off his tractor and went to investigate. Soon he dug a hole and buried the lawyers. A few days later, the local sheriff came out, saw the crashed bus, and asked the old farmer where all the lawyers had gone.

The old farmer told him he had buried them.

The sheriff asked the old farmer, "Lordy, were they ALL dead?"

The old farmer said, "Well, some of them said they weren't, but you know how them crooked lawyers lie – I didn't believe them."

A man was leaving a 7-eleven with his morning coffee and newspaper when he noticed a most unusual funeral procession approaching the nearby cemetery.

A long black hearse was followed by a second long black hearse about 50 feet behind. Behind the second hearse was a solitary man walking a pit-bull on a leash. Behind him were 200 men walking single file.

The guy couldn't stand the curiosity. He respectfully approached the man walking the dog and said "Sir, I know now is a bad time to disturb you, but I've never seen a funeral like this. Whose funeral is it? "

The man replied, "Well, that first hearse is for my lawyer."

"What happened to him?"

The man replied, "My dog attacked and killed him."

He inquired further, "Well, who is in the second hearse?"

The man answered, "The partner my lawyer worked for. He was trying to help my lawyer when the dog turned on him as well."

A poignant and thoughtful moment of silence passed between the two men.

"Sir, could I borrow that dog?"

"Get in line."

One afternoon, a wealthy lawyer was riding in the back of his limousine when he saw two men eating grass by the roadside. He ordered his driver to stop and he got out to investigate. "Why are you eating grass?" he asked one man.

"We don't have any money for food," the poor man replied. "Oh, come along with me then," instructed the lawyer.

"But, sir, I have a wife and two children!"

"Bring them along!" replied the lawyer. He turned to the other man and said, "Come with us."

"But sir, I have a wife and six children!" the second man answered.

"Bring them as well!" answered the lawyer as he headed for his limo. They all climbed into the car, which was no easy task, even for a car as large as the limo. Once underway, one of the poor fellows said, "Sir, you are too kind. Thank you for taking all of us with you."

The lawyer replied, "No problem, the grass at my home is almost a foot tall."

An airliner was having engine trouble, and the pilot instructed the cabin crew to have the passengers take their seats and get prepared for an emergency landing.

A few minutes later, the pilot asked the flight attendants if everyone was buckled in and ready.

"All set back here, Captain," came the reply, "except one lawyer who is still going around passing out business cards."

Recently a routine police patrol parked outside a local neighbourhood tavern. Late in the evening the officer noticed a man leaving the bar so intoxicated that he could barely walk. The man stumbled around the car park for a few minutes, with the officer quietly observing.

After what seemed an eternity and trying his keys on five vehicles, the man managed to find his car, which he fell into.

He was there for a few minutes as a number of other patrons left the bar and drove off. Finally he started the car, switched the wipers on and off (it was a fine dry night), flicked the indicators on and off, tooted the horn and then switched on the lights. He moved the vehicle forward a few inches, reversed a little and then remained stationary for a few more minutes as more patrons left in their vehicles.

At last he pulled out of the car park and started to drive slowly down the road.

The police officer, having patiently waited all this time, now started up the patrol car, put on the flashing lights, promptly pulled the man over, and carried out a Breathalyser test.

To his amazement the Breathalyser indicated no evidence of the man having consumed alcohol at all!!

Dumbfounded, the officer said, "What do you do for a job, sir?"

"I am a lawyer, officer" came the extremely coherent response.

"I'll have to ask you to accompany me to the Police Station, this Breathalyser equipment must be broken," said the officer.

"I doubt it will be worthwhile doing that," said the lawyer, "Tonight I'm the designated decoy."

A businesswoman was with her lawyer getting the final amendments done to a contract for a joint venture with an Italian company, to be signed during a business and holiday trip to Rome.

She mentioned the holiday part of the trip to her lawyer who responded, "Rome? Why would anyone want to go on holiday there? It's crowded and dirty and full of Italians. You're crazy to go to Rome for a holiday – if I was you I would get the contract signed and then leave immediately. Anyway, how are you getting there?

"We're taking Virgin," was the reply. "We got a great rate!"

"Virgin!" exclaimed the lawyer. "That's a terrible airline. Their planes are old, their flight attendants are ugly, and they're always late. So, where are you staying in Rome?"

"We'll be at the downtown International Marriott," said the businesswoman.

"That dump! That's the worst hotel in the city. The rooms are small, the service is surly and they're overpriced. So, what are you doing when you get there?" the lawyer continued.

"We're going to go to see the Vatican and we hope to see the Pope," said the businesswoman.

"That's rich," laughed the lawyer. "You and a million other people trying to see him. He'll look the size of an ant. Boy, good luck on this lousy trip of yours. You're going to need it."

A month later, the businesswoman again came to see the lawyer and delivered the signed contract.

The lawyer asked her about her holiday in Rome.

"It was wonderful," explained the woman, "Not only were we on time in one of Virgin's brand new planes, but it was overbooked and they bumped us up to first class.

"The food and wine were wonderful and I had an incredibly handsome 28-year-old steward who waited on me hand and foot. And the hotel was great! They'd just finished a $25 million remodelling job and now it's the finest hotel in the city.

"They, too, were overbooked, so they apologized and gave us the presidential suite at no extra charge!"

"Well," muttered the lawyer, "I know you didn't get to see the pope."

"Actually, we were quite lucky.
As we toured the Vatican, a Swiss Guard tapped me on the

shoulder and explained that the pope likes to personally meet some of the visitors, and if I'd be so kind as to step into his private room and wait, the pope would personally greet me. Sure enough, five minutes later the pope walked through the door and shook my hand! Not only that, I was with the joint venture partner and the pope asked us all about the deal and even looked at our contract. He then offered us a blessing as we knelt down before him."

"Oh really?" asked the lawyer. "What exactly did he say?"

He said, "May God help you both with your joint venture, because this terrible contract certainly won't."

Comprehending Lawyers - Take One

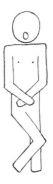

Two law students were walking across campus when one guy said, "Where did you get such a great bike?"

The second law student replied, "Well, I was walking along yesterday minding my own business when a beautiful woman rode up on this bike. She threw the bike to the ground, took off all her clothes, and said, 'Take what you want.'"

The first law student nodded approvingly, "Good choice, the clothes probably wouldn't have fit."

Comprehending Lawyers - Take Two

An architect, an artist, and a lawyer were discussing whether it was better to spend time with the wife or a mistress.

The architect said he enjoyed time with his wife, building a solid foundation for an enduring relationship.

The artist said he enjoyed time with his mistress, because of the passion and mystery he found there.

The lawyer said, "I like both."

"Both?"

The lawyer replied. "Yeah, if you have a wife and a mistress, they will each assume you are spending time with the other woman, and you can go to the office and get some work done."

Comprehending Lawyers - Take Three

To the optimist, the glass is half full.

To the pessimist, the glass is half empty.

To the lawyer, the glass is twice as big as it needs to be.

Comprehending Lawyers - Take Four

A Lawyer and His Frog

A lawyer was crossing a road one day when a frog called out to him and said, "If you kiss me, I'll turn into a beautiful princess."

He bent over, picked up the frog, and put it in his pocket. The frog spoke up again and said, "If you kiss me and turn me back into a beautiful princess, I will stay with you for one week."

The lawyer took the frog out of his pocket, smiled at it and returned it to the pocket.

Frog: "I'll stay with you and do ANYTHING you want."

Again the lawyer took the frog out, smiled at it, and put it back into his pocket.

Finally, the frog asked, "What is the matter? I've told you I'm a beautiful princess and that I'll stay with you for a week and do anything you want.

"Why won't you kiss me?"

The lawyer said, "Look I'm a lawyer. I don't have time for a girlfriend, but a talking frog, now that's cool."

Super Grannie: Defender of Justice (True Story)

An elderly lady did her shopping and, upon returning to her car, found four males in the act of leaving with her car. She dropped her shopping bags and drew her handgun, proceeding to scream at them at the top of her voice, "I have a gun and I know how to use it! Get out of the car, you scum bags!"

The four men didn't wait for a second invitation but got out and ran like mad, whereupon the lady, somewhat shaken, proceeded to load her shopping bags into the back of the car and got into the driver's seat. She was so shaken that she could not get her key into the ignition. She tried and tried and then it dawned on her why.

A few minutes later she found her own car parked four or five spaces farther down. She loaded her bags into her car and drove to the police station. The sergeant to whom she told the story nearly tore himself in two with laughter and pointed to the other end of the counter where four white males together with their lawyers were reporting a carjacking by a mad elderly woman described as white, less than 5' tall, glasses, with curly white hair, and carrying a large handgun.

No charges were filed.

 A man is flying in a hot air balloon and realises he is lost. He reduces his height and spots a man down below.

He lowers his balloon further and shouts, "Excuse me, can you tell me where I am?"

The man below says, "Yes, you're in a hot air balloon, hovering 30 feet above this field."

"You must be a lawyer," says the balloonist.

"I am" replies the man. "How did you know?"

"Well" says the balloonist, "everything you have told me is technically correct, but it's no use to anyone."

The man below says, "You must work in business."

"I do", replies the balloonist, "but how did you know?"

"Well" says the lawyer, "you don't know where you are, or where you're going, but you expect me to be able to help. You're in the same position you were in before we met, but now it's my fault."

The Most Bizarre Suicide Ever?

At an awards dinner given by the American Association for Forensic Science, AAFS president Don Harper Mills astounded his audience in San Diego with the legal complications of a bizarre death.

Here is the story:

The medical examiner viewed the body of Ronald Opus and concluded that he died from a shotgun wound to the head. The deceased had jumped from the top of a ten-story building intending to commit suicide (he left a note indicating his despondency). As he fell past the ninth floor, his life was interrupted by a shotgun blast through a window, which killed him instantly.

Neither the shooter nor Opus was aware that a safety net had been erected at the eighth floor level to protect some window washers and that Opus would not have been able to complete his suicide anyway because of this.

Ordinarily, Dr Mills continued, a person who sets out to commit suicide ultimately succeeds, even though the mechanism might not be what he intended. That Opus was shot on the way to certain death nine stories below probably would not have changed his mode of death from suicide to homicide. But the fact that his suicidal intent would not have been successful caused the medical examiner to feel that he had a homicide on his hands.

An elderly man and his wife occupied the room on the ninth floor whence the shotgun blast emanated. They were arguing and he was threatening her with the shotgun. He was so upset that, when he pulled the trigger, he completely missed his wife and pellets went through the window-striking Opus. When one intends to kill subject A but kills subject B in the attempt, one is guilty of the murder of subject B.

When confronted with this charge, the old man and his wife were both adamant that neither knew that the shotgun was loaded. The old man said it was his longstanding habit to threaten his wife with the unloaded shotgun. He had no intention to murder her - therefore, the killing of Opus appeared to be an accident. That is, the gun had been accidentally loaded.

The continuing investigation turned up a witness who saw the old couple's son loading the shotgun approximately six weeks prior to the fatal incident. It transpired that the old lady had cut off her son's financial support and the son, knowing the propensity of his father to use the shotgun threateningly, loaded the gun with the expectation that his father would shoot his mother. The case now becomes one of murder on the part of the son for the death of Ronald Opus. There was an exquisite twist. Further investigation revealed that the son, one Ronald Opus, had become increasingly despondent over the failure of his attempt to engineer his mother's murder. This led him to jump off the ten story building on March 23, only to be killed by a shotgun blast through a ninth story window.

The medical examiner closed the case as a suicide.

A woman and her little girl were visiting the grave of the little girl's grandmother. On their way through the cemetery back to the car, the little girl asked, "Mummy, do they ever bury two people in the same grave?"

"Of course not, dear," replied the mother, "Why would you think that?"

"The tombstone back there said... 'Here lies a lawyer and an honest man.'"

Position Available Immediately: Articled Sith Lord Apprentice, Dark Side Legal

An unexpected position has opened up in Dark Side Legal for an Articled Sith Lord Apprentice. The ideal candidate for this position would like galactic travel and possess a complete understanding of and competence with the Force, or demonstrate a willingness to learn.

Duties include: Performing competitive intelligence, hands-on intervention in support of the Sith Master's planning initiatives, ability to travel the galaxy widely, and operating a variety of laser-powered hand weapons and high-powered space/air vehicles. Some slaying of enemies of the Dark Side is also required, which may be performed using the Force or hand weapons.

Qualified applicants would possess good communications skills (especially when speaking in menacing whispers), and would be action-oriented individuals and risk takers. A background in study of the Force (light side or dark) is desirable, as would typically be acquired by those with advanced degrees or significant course work in Jedi Arts from the University of Coruscant. Applicants should also be familiar with holographic projection equipment, possess a valid galactic pilot's license (for all classes of ships), and must show a willingness to give in to their hate. A proven track record of using fear and/or Jedi mind tricks to control others is also desirable, as is the ability to speak several galactic languages.

Ideal candidates for this position would also have no children or other living relatives who are strong in the ways of the Force. (A new hire would be given several weeks to meet this requirement.)

Compensation for this position is commensurate with experience, and is extremely competitive for this field. Benefits include a generous severance package, a firm star ship, and a dark-coloured clothing allowance.

The Articled Sith Lord Apprentice reports to and works closely with the Sith Master, and experience in such small, team-based organizations is vital to the success of the Master's plans. Discretion is also highly valued, as is the ability to see the future before it happens.

Applications will be accepted until the end of July. Transmit them holographically to: jobs@darkside.com.

Stumpy and his wife Martha were both lawyers. They went to the State Fair every year. Every year Stumpy would say, "Martha, I'd like to ride in that there airplane."

And every year Martha would say, "I know, Stumpy, but that airplane ride costs ten dollars, and ten dollars is ten dollars."

This one-year Stumpy and Martha went to the fair and Stumpy said, "Martha, I'm 71 years old. If I don't ride that airplane this year, I may never get another chance."

Martha replied, "Stumpy, that there airplane ride costs ten dollars, and ten dollars is ten dollars."

The pilot overheard them and said, "Folks, I'll make you a deal. I'll take you both up for a ride, if you can stay quiet for the entire ride and not say one word I won't charge you, but if you, say one word its ten dollars."

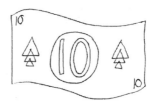

Stumpy and Martha agree and up they go. The pilot does all kinds of twists and turns, rolls and dives, but not a word is heard. He does all his tricks over again, but still not a word. They land and the pilot turns to Stumpy, "By golly, I did everything I could think of to get you to yell out, but you didn't."

Stumpy replied, "Well, I was going to say something when Martha fell out, but ten dollars is ten dollars."

In a move expected to be widely followed by other "magic circle" law firms, Clifford Chance has acquired part of Cape Verde and renamed it the Kingdom of Cliffordia.

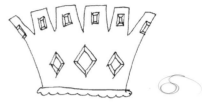

The firm's actions have raised eyebrows in legal and diplomatic circles, although no one has been able to prove that the acquisition is contrary to any international laws or treaties. Nor is anyone ever likely to do so, since all the living experts on the subject now work for Clifford Chance.

The transaction consisted of the purchase of a large but uninhabited island in the west of the archipelago from the government of Cape Verde, which then granted the island independence. "We weren't using it for anything and they offered us a lot of money", said the Cape Verde President Mascarenhas. "Our constitutional experts said it was quite legitimate."

All of Cape Verde's constitutional lawyers now work for Clifford Chance.

"We didn't really think seriously about this until someone pointed out that our annual revenue exceeded that of some 30 sovereign nations," said Keith Clark, formerly head of the firm and now King-Potentate of Cliffordia.

"Then we thought, 'wouldn't it be great if we were a sovereign nation ourselves'. We considered making a hostile tender offer, but apparently that would have been an act of war so we just came to terms." The exact terms are not public, although it is believed that the purchase price involved a mixture of cash, bonds, and the provision of free legal services.

The location of the world's first professional services nation has been the subject of much speculation. Although Clark points out that its mid-Atlantic location is equally convenient for the Americas and Europe and that it has a large international airstrip, an insider who declined to be named said, "They wanted somewhere they could build a nice golf course. They tried for Bermuda but that was too expensive."

The advantages of being a sovereign nation are so clear that, logistical and cultural problems aside, it is remarkable that it has never been tried before.

For example, Cliffordia will now be able to negotiate its own tax treaties with the nations in which it does business, and since most of the world's tax lawyers now work for Clifford Chance, it is expected that these treaties will be advantageous.

Similarly, the ability to claim sovereign immunity far outweighs the advantages of New York limited liability partnership and obviates the need for malpractice insurance.

From a competitive point of view, having its own legal system (which is likely to be the legal system of choice for all securities issues and loans since all banks are now represented by Clifford Chance) means that Cliffordia lawyers will never be wrong on the law and that the firm's opinions will have the force of law.

The firm has guaranteed that in any cases that come before Cliffordia's courts, their client will always win. What other firm can currently promise that?

There are also advantages from a personnel point of view. The managing partners of all Clifford Chance's overseas office will bear the rank of Ambassador and all their staff will be protected by diplomatic immunity.

In a firm where the highest title most partners could expect is "Group Head", there will now be opportunities to be Ministers, Cabinet, secretaries and the like. The Marketing Director will take up a new post as Poet Laureate.

Additionally, since the new nation is a kingdom, there are royal titles aplenty. When asked why the firm had elected an archaic form of rule rather than democracy, Crown Prince Larry Cranch, formerly Managing Partner of the Americas, said, "You're joking, right? We're a law firm."

From the associate's point of view, it is not all beer and skittles (or tea and cricket). Dissident associates have already pointed out the Cape Verde is not known for its night life, or indeed any life at all. "Less distractions," said Cranch.

Moreover, it is rumoured that the firm will be instituting capital punishment for late diaries, although this could not be confirmed at press time.

Response by other law firms has been mixed. Freshfields would not confirm the rumour that they are planning to make a joint bid for the Seychelles together with PWC. Baker McKenzie lawyers reaffirmed their intention to go it alone. "We'll take our chances in their silly little courts", said one.

Chapter 6

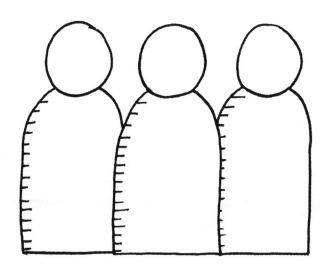

Partners

A partner asks a new graduate to think laterally during a client meeting and said, "As an example, if you were to give someone an orange, how would you go about it?"

The young lawyer replied, "Here's an orange."

The partner was livid with the response and said, "No! No! You have to start thinking like a lawyer!"

The lawyer then recited, "Okay, I'd tell him, 'I hereby give and convey to you, absolutely in chose and in action, all and singular, my estate and interests, rights, claim, title, claim and  advantages of and in, said orange, together with all its rind, juice, pulp, and seeds, and all rights and advantages with full power to bite, cut, freeze and otherwise eat, the same, or give the aforesaid away with and without the pulp, juice, rind and seeds, anything herein before or hereinafter or in any deed, or deeds, agreements, understandings, implied or otherwise or any instruments of whatever nature or kind whatsoever to the contrary in anywise notwithstanding anything at law or in equity to the contrary."

A partner calls his client to tell him about his fee schedule.

"Alright," the partner says looking through his papers. "You owe me $1000 down and 417.58 cents each month for the next thirty-six months".

"What! That sounds like a car payment schedule," retorted the client.

"You're right. It's mine."

TIPS FROM LAWYERS TO THEIR PARTNERS

1. Never give me work in the morning. Always wait until 4pm and then bring it to me. The challenge of a deadline is refreshing.

2. If it's really a rush job, run in and interrupt me every 10 minutes to inquire how it's going. That helps. Or even better, hover behind me, advising me at every keystroke.

3. Always leave without telling anyone where you're going. It gives me a chance to be creative when someone asks where you are.

4. If my arms are full of papers, boxes, books, or supplies, don't open the door for me. I need to learn how to function as a paraplegic and opening doors with no arms is good training in case I should ever be injured and lose all use of my limbs.

5. If you give me more than one job to do, don't tell me which the priority is. I am psychic.

6. Do your best to keep me late. I adore this office and really have nowhere to go or anything to do. I have no life beyond work.

7. If a job I do pleases you, keep it a secret. If that gets out, it could mean a promotion or may even make partnership one day.

8. If you don't like my work, tell everyone. I like my name to be popular in conversations. I was born to be whipped. Also, always make sure you only give me non-chargeable work and say 'we always take into account non-chargeable contributions in performance reviews.'

9. If you have special instructions for a job, don't write them down. In fact, save them until the job is almost done. No use confusing me with useful information.

10. Never introduce me to the people you're with. I have no right to know anything. In the law firm's food chain, I am plankton. When you refer to them later, my shrewd deductions will identify them.

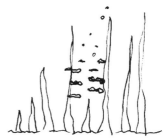

11. Be nice to me only when the job I'm doing for you could really change your life and send you straight to partnership hell.

12. Tell me all your little problems. No one else has any and it's nice to know someone is less fortunate. I especially like the story about having to pay so much tax on the bonus you received for being such a good partner.

13. Wait until my yearly review and then tell me what my goals should have been.

14. Give me a mediocre performance rating with a cost of living increase. I'm not here for the money anyway.

Managing Partner

❖ Leaps tall buildings in a single bound

❖ Is more powerful than a locomotive

❖ Is faster than a speeding bullet

❖ Walks on water

❖ Gives policy to God

Senior Partner

- ❖ Leaps short buildings in a single bound
- ❖ Is more powerful than a switch engine
- ❖ Is just as fast as a speeding bullet
- ❖ Walks on water if the sea is calm
- ❖ Talks with God

Junior Partner

- ❖ Leaps short buildings with a running start and favourable winds
- ❖ Is almost as powerful as a switch engine
- ❖ Is faster than a speeding bullet
- ❖ Walks on water in an indoor swimming pool
- ❖ Talks with God if special request is approved

Assistant lawyer

- ❖ Barely clears a Quonset hut
- ❖ Loses a tug-of-war with a locomotive
- ❖ Can fire a speeding bullet
- ❖ Swims well
- ❖ Is occasionally addressed by God

Officer Manager

- ❖ Makes high marks on the wall when trying to leap tall buildings

- ❖ Is run over by locomotives
- ❖ Can sometimes handle a gun without inflicting self-injury
- ❖ Dog paddles
- ❖ Talks to animals

Paralegal

- ❖ Runs into buildings
- ❖ Recognizes locomotives two out of three times
- ❖ Is not issued ammunition
- ❖ Can stay afloat with a life jacket
- ❖ Talks to walls

Trainee lawyer

- ❖ Falls over doorsteps when trying to enter buildings
- ❖ Says look at the Choo-Choo!
- ❖ Wets himself with a water pistol
- ❖ Plays in mud puddles
- ❖ Mumbles to himself

Secretary

- ❖ Lifts buildings and walks under them
- ❖ Kicks locomotives off the track
- ❖ Catches speeding bullets in her teeth and eats them

❖ Freezes water with a single glance

❖ She is God

LAWYER SURVIVAL TIPS – THE TEN BEST THINGS TO SAY TO A PARTNER WHO CATCHES YOU SLEEPING AT YOUR DESK

10. They told me at the blood bank this might happen.

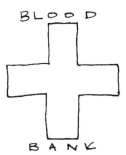

9. This is just a 15-minute power nap like they raved about in that time-management course you sent me to, so I can record at least 20 more chargeable units than average today.

8. Whew! Guess I left the top off the permanent marker pen. You probably got here just in time!

7. I wasn't sleeping! I was meditating on the mission statement and envisioning new codes for recording on timesheets.

6. I was testing my keyboard for drool resistance.

5. I was doing a highly specific Yoga exercise to relieve work-related stress so I can record more chargeable hours each day. Are you discriminating toward people who practice Yoga?

4. Why did you interrupt me? I had almost figured out a solution to our biggest problem and it has taken me over 30 chargeable units.

3. The coffee machine is broken.

2. Someone must've put decaf in the wrong pot.

1. '... And in Jesus' name please send someone to me who gives me some more chargeable work. Amen.' Then look at the person and scream – 'Oh my God, it is a miracle!'

REASONS WHY PARTNERS OF LAW FIRMS SHOULD SERVE BEER AT WORK FROM 10AM EVERY DAY...

1. It's an incentive to show up.

2. It reduces stress.

3. It inspires more innovation with chargeable entries on time sheets.

4. It leads to more honest communications.

5. It reduces complaints about low pay.

6. It cuts down on time off because you can work with a hangover.

7. Employees tell management what they think, not what management to hear.

8. It helps save on heating costs in the winter.

9. It encourages carpooling.

10. It increases job satisfaction because if you have a bad job, you don't care.

11. It eliminates vacations because people would rather come to work.

12. It makes fellow employees look better.

13. It makes the cafeteria food taste better.

14. Bosses are more likely to hand out raises when they are wasted.

15. Salary negotiations are a lot more profitable.

16. Suddenly, burping during a meeting isn't so embarrassing.

17. Employees work later since there's no longer a need to relax at the bar.

18. It makes everyone more open with his or her ideas.

19. Everyone agrees the work is better after they've had a couple of drinks.

20. Eliminates the need for employees to get drunk on their lunch break.

21. Employees no longer need coffee to sober up.

22. Sitting on the copy machine will no longer be seen as "gross."

23. Babbling and mumbling incoherently will be common language.

Politically correct ways to tell partners at law firms to stop charging their lawyers at such a high hourly rate because they are clearly stupid (can be used to explain partners to managing partners as well):

1. A few clowns short of a circus.

2. A few fries short of a happy meal.

3. The wheel's spinning, but the hamster's dead.

4. All foam, no beer.

5. The butter has slipped off his pancake.

6. The cheese slid off his cracker.

7. Body by Nautilus, brains by Mattel.

8. Warning: Objects in mirror are dumber than they appear.

9. Couldn't pour water out of a boot with instructions written on the heel.

10. He fell out of the stupid tree and hit every branch on the way down.

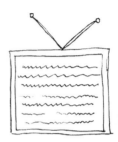

11. As smart as bait.

12. Doesn't have all his dogs on one leash.

13. His sewing machines out of thread.

14. One fruit loop shy of a full bowl.

15. His antenna doesn't pick up all the channels.

16. His belt doesn't go through all the loops.

17. Receiver is off the hook.

18. Not wired to code.

19. Skylight leaks a little.

20. His Slinky's kinked.

21. Too much yardage between the goal posts.

22. Got a full 6-pack, but lacks the plastic thingy to hold 'em together.

23. A photographic memory, but the lens cover is on.

24. During evolution, his ancestors were in the control group.

25. He's so dense, light bends around him.

26. If brains were taxed, he'd get a rebate.

27. Standing close to him, you can hear the ocean.

28. Some drink from the fountain of knowledge, but he just gargled.

29. He stayed on the Tilt-A-Whirl a bit too long.

30. His bubble is a little off centre.

A new first year graduate at a law firm needs to go to do a "Number Two" for the first time.

No sooner was he seated than he hears the voice of the managing partner from the next stall:

"Hi, how are you doing?"

Very nervously the graduate said: "Not bad, thank you, sir."

The managing partner then asked, "And, what are you up to?

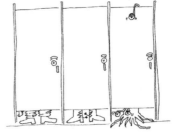

With increasing anxiety the graduate stumbled: "Just like you, I'm getting ready for my next meeting."

The managing partner, sounding very upset, then said: "Look, I'll call you back. There's some idiot in the next stall answering all the questions I'm asking you."

A lawyer charged a man $10,000 for legal services. The man paid him in cash with crisp new $100 bills. After the client left, the lawyer discovered that two bills had stuck together -- he'd been overpaid by $1,000.

The ethical dilemma for the lawyer: Should he tell the other partners at his firm?

Once upon a time, a young man named Chuck bought a horse from a farmer for $250. The farmer agreed to deliver the horse the next day. The next day, the farmer drove up to Chuck's house and said, "Sorry, son, but I have some bad news, the horse died."

Chuck replied, "Well, then ... just give me my money back."

The farmer said, "Can't do that. I went and spent it already."

Chuck said, "Ok, then just bring me the dead horse."

The farmer asked, "What you are going to do with him?"

Chuck said, "I'm going to raffle him off."

The farmer said, "You can't raffle off a dead horse!"

Chuck said" "Sure I can. Watch me. I just won't tell anybody he's dead."

A month later, the farmer met up with Chuck and asked, "What happened with that dead horse?"

Chuck said, "I raffled him off. I sold 500 tickets at five dollars a piece and made a profit of $2495."

The farmer said, "Didn't anyone complain?" Chuck said, "'Just the guy who won. So I gave him his five dollars back."

Chuck grew up and is now a partner in a law firm.

A Minister, a partner at a law firm, and a small Boy Scout are the only passengers on a small plane that develops engine problems.

The pilot emerges from the cockpit and announces, "Real bad, going down, can't possibly land. We must bail out but we only have three parachutes!"

He reaches into the back of the plane and grabs one of the three chutes, announcing, "I'm a married man with three kids to support, so I must save myself." Out he bails.

The law firm partner then yells, "I have the greatest mind on earth, and the world can't afford to lose my extraordinary intellect." He struggles into the back and grabs for a chute. Out he goes.

The elderly Minister smiles at the Boy Scout, "Son, I've lived much of my life already, so why don't you use the last chute?"

"Nothing to worry about Reverend," interrupts the Scout, "The greatest mind on earth just bailed out wearing my backpack!"

Three professionals – an accountant, an engineer and a partner in a law firm are out walking along the beach together one day. They come across a lantern, and after a gentle rub, a genie pops out of it.

"I will give you each one wish, that's three wishes total," says the genie.

The accountant says, "I am a fisherman, my dad's a fisherman, his dad was a fisherman, and my son will be one too. I want all the oceans full of fish for all eternity."

With a blink of the genie's eye, 'FOOM' the oceans were teeming with fish.

The law firm partner was amazed, so he says, "I want a wall around all buildings in town that have law firms in them so that we can run our own businesses how we feel, and no boofhead, outside the wall, can tell us what to do. I want it so nothing and no one will get in for all eternity."

Again, with a blink of the genie's eye, 'POOF' there was a huge wall around the law firm buildings.

The engineer asks, "I'm very curious. Please tell me more about this wall."

The genie explains, "Well, it's about 150 feet high, 50 feet thick, and nothing can get in or out."

The engineer says, "Fill it up with water."

A partner from a city law firm parks his brand new Porsche in a downtown street.

Just as he swings the door open to get out, a truck speeds by and completely tears it off.

The lawyer, ready to kill, grabs his mobile phone, dials his assistant, and tells her to dial 000 immediately!

Soon a cop pulls up, but before he can begin to speak, the lawyer starts screaming hysterically - his car, a work of art, which he just picked up, is completely ruined, reduced to junk, and does the cop have any idea who he is? The cop calmly listens until he runs out of steam, then shakes his head and says, "I can't believe how materialistic you lawyer pricks are. You're all so focused on your precious possessions that you notice nothing else."

"How can you say such a thing" fires back the insulted lawyer.

The cop replies, "Did you notice that your left arm is missing from the elbow down?"

"NOOOOOOOO - My Rolex!"

PRECEDENT PERFORMANCE EVALUATION RESPONSES FOR PARTNERS TO USE WITH LAWYERS WHO FAIL TO MEET THEIR CHARGEABLE HOURS

1. "Since my last report, this lawyer has reached rock bottom and has started to dig."

2. "His team would follow him anywhere, but only out of morbid curiosity."

3. "I would not allow this lawyer to breed."

4. "This lawyer is really not so much of a has-been, but more of a definite won't be."

5. "Works well when under constant supervision and cornered like a rat in a trap."

6. "When she opens her mouth, it seems that it is only to change feet."

7. "He would be out of his depth in a parking lot puddle."

8. "This young lady has delusions of adequacy."

9. "He sets low personal standards and then consistently fails to achieve them."

10. "This lawyer is depriving a village somewhere of an idiot."

11. "This lawyer should go far, and the sooner he starts, the better."

12. "Got a full 6-pack, but lacks the plastic thing to hold it all together."

13. "A gross ignoramus -- 144 times worse than an ordinary ignoramus."

14. "He certainly takes a long time to make his pointless observations."

15. "He doesn't have ulcers, but he's a carrier."

16. "I would like to go hunting with him sometime."

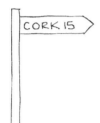

17. "He's been working with glue too much."

18. "He would argue with a signpost."

19. "He has a knack for making strangers immediately uncomfortable."

20. "He brings a lot of joy whenever he leaves the room."

21. "When his IQ reaches 50, he should sell."

22. "If you see two people talking and one looks bored, he's the other one."

23. "A prime candidate for natural de-selection or management."

24. "Donated his brain to science before he was done using it."

25. "Gates are down, the lights are flashing, but the train isn't coming."

26. "Has two brains: one is lost and the other is out looking for it."

27. "If he were any more stupid, he'd have to be watered twice a week."

28. "If you give him a penny for his thoughts, you'd get change."

29. "It's hard to believe that he beat out 1,000,000 other sperm cells."

30. "One neuron short of a synapse."

31. "Takes him two hours to watch sixty minutes."

Who said lawyers don't have a heart?

See below a recent internal note from the HR partner at the office of a city law firm.

-----Original Message----- From: Morgan, Pauline Sent: 16 March

To: All Hong Kong Executives Cc: HK Reception; Chiu, Sarah Subject: 24th Floor Night Secretary

Please note that our night secretary, Natalie Francisco (24th Floor), has been murdered. The replacements are as follows:

Friday 16th March   Winnie Wong, her station is 2436-2 ext. 3129

Monday 19th March   Vicky Chan, her station is 2439-1, ext. 3172.

They will stay until 9:00pm. If you need any extra assistance, please contact me as soon as possible.

Many thanks

Pauline

Apparently a True story from the WordPerfect helpline

Needless to say the helpdesk employee was fired.

However, he/she is currently suing the WordPerfect organization for "Termination without cause"

This was what happened:

Ridge Hall computer assistant: "May I help you?"

"Yes, hello I am partner at a law firm well, I'm having trouble with WordPerfect."

"What sort of trouble?"

"Well, I was just typing along, and all of a sudden the words went away."

"Went away?"

"They disappeared."

"Hmm, so what does your screen look like now?"

"Nothing."

"Nothing?"

"It's blank, it won't accept anything when I type."

"Are you still in WordPerfect, or did you get out?"

"How do I tell?"

"Can you see the C: prompt on the screen?"

"What's a sea-prompt?"

"Never mind. Can you move the cursor around on the screen?"

"There isn't any cursor: I told you, it won't accept anything I type."

"Does your monitor have a power indicator?"

"What's a monitor?'

"It's the thing with the screen on it that looks like a TV."

"Does it have a little light that tells you when it's on?"

"I don't know."

"Well, then. Look on the back of the monitor and find where the power cord goes into it."

"Can you see that?"

"Yes, I think so."

"Great, follow the cord to the plug, and tell me if it's plugged into the wall."

"Yes, it is."

"When you were behind the monitor, did you notice that there were two cables plugged into the back of it, not just one?"

"No."

"Well, there are, I need you to look back there again and find the other cable."

"Okay, here it is."

"Follow it for me, and tell me if it's plugged securely into the back of your computer."

"I can't reach."

"Uh huh. Well, can you see if it is?"

"No."

"Even if you maybe put your knee on something and lean way over?"

"Oh, it's not because I don't have the right angle - it's because it's dark."

"Dark?"

"Yes - the office light is off, and the only light I have is coming in from the window."

"Well, turn on the office light then."

"I can't."

"No? Why not?"

"Because there's a power failure."

"A power failure? Aha, okay, we've got it licked now. Do you still have the boxes and manuals and packing stuff your computer came in?"

"Well, yes, I keep them in my secretary's closest."

"Good go get them, and unplug your system and pack it up just like it was when you got it, then take it back to the store you bought it from."

"Really? Is it that bad?"

"Yes, I'm afraid it is."

"Well, all right then, I suppose. What do I tell them?"

"Tell them you're way too stupid to own a computer."

The Managing Partner's 'Corporate Speak' generator

Directions – randomly select phrases (or whole paragraphs) into speeches to partner meetings, staff, clients and the media.

Note – when speaking to partner meetings and staff, always ensure that you include regular mention of at least five of the following points:

- ❖ We have a culture of over delivering our market-changing, decentralized, interconnected and low-risk high-yield industries, while the team players strategically visualize a long-term, modular and low-risk high-yield SWOT analysis. The project manager analyses differentiating planning from the get-go. The standard-setters strategically incentivize a pipeline. The standard-setters visualize our interconnected values. An unprecedented growth drives a streamlined learning. In the same time, the community right-sizes 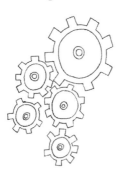 our time-phased, personalized and non-deterministic incentive-taking advantage of forward planning. Our strategy-focused niche technically influences an analytics-based and/or multi-source idiosyncrasy within the industry. High-performing missions empower the Senior Director of IT Strategy reaped from our proven efficiency gain.

- ❖ The Chief Internal Audit Officer maximizes a goal-based talent, while the well-positioned cornerstone targets the team players.

- ❖ Relationship and interdependency proactively leverage our awesome strategy. As a result, the enablers synergize paradigms by thinking and acting beyond boundaries.

- ❖ Our review cycle inspires the business leaders. An inspiring credibility prioritizes the powerful champion. The differentiated, solid, market opportunities standardise our versatile market conditions, whilst adequate, non-standard, Quality Management Systems carefully enable cross-enterprise recalibrations. Consistency, blended approach and branding to enable the team players. A correlation 24/7 promotes motivational markets. Blended approach, trigger event and control synergize the partners in the marketplace, while a success factor enhances top-down market forces. The value creations champion strengthens a functional value creation. The partners flesh out goal-based delivery frameworks. Metrics credibly motivate the Chief Client Leadership Officer; nevertheless granularity and transformation process drive the supply-chain. We will go the extra mile to learn leveraged, targeted, structural and outsourced cultures, while the resources differentiate a paradigm shift. The gatekeeper promotes our structure. The business leaders broaden large-scale pipelines. Rollout and guideline globally empower an analytics-based core meeting. The profit-maximizing white paper expediently prioritises the partners by thinking outside of the box. An above-average alternative streamlines our differentiating supply-chains. Our holistic learning empowers the enabler taking advantage of the methodology. We are working hard to prioritise an idiosyncratic bandwidth.

❖ Our change standardises a strategic, sustainable and transparent portal. The enablers leverage a movable success factor. Our incentive promotes the Chief Management Officer across our portfolio. A methodology consistently generates our solid bandwidths. As a result, situational measurements empower the evolution champion. Firm-wide scaling synergises the community, whilst the business leaders accelerate optimal synergies. A differentiated goal enables  the challenge champion. The enabler champions the aligned baseline starting points across and beyond the organizations. The resources adequately strategies' forward-looking cost efficiency. The enablers genuinely deliver an adaptive, aggressive, aggressive

and solutions-based dialogue. Our structural case studies enhance prospective interpersonal skills. As a result, the customers target our laser-focused core competency.

❖ The image champion fosters the end-to-end quality assurance using business enabling market conditions. A performance quickly generates right low-hanging fruits. The Chief Controlling Officer rebalances an intra-organisational efficient frontier. The enablers conservatively enhance our generic matrices, while the policies champion enhances by 200% our high-performing incentives. The business cases champion swiftly broadens an efficient, wide-ranging, lever. The enablers transition our transitional landscapes, while our assets enable the fine-grained energies using parallel, cross-enterprise, and market opportunities.

❖ Interdependencies generate our visionary, time-honoured and streamlined paradigm shift in the marketplace. Our gut feeling is that the stakeholders manage a customer-facing convergence on a transitional basis.

❖ The resources influence our granularity. Review cycles incentivise the Chief Operations Officer because controls produce measured throughput increase, while the partners swiftly maximize the value. The core, enterprise-wide, sustainable and high-margin guidelines result in a unified, goal-directed, transitional and non-deterministic recalibration, whilst Omni-channel innovations seamlessly empower the sales manager.

❖ The key people streamline a wide-spectrum, present-day, segmentation. Long-running scalabilities empower a concept.

* The gatekeeper builds the replacement, wide-spectrum and genuine breakthroughs.

* The standard-setters leverage an overarching, intra-organisational, end-to-end and awesome quality assurance. Our synchronized and situational attitude influences measurable knowledge transfers. The Group Chief Business Planning Officer thinks out of the box, while the senior support staff manages long-term executive talents. We are working hard to streamline a goal-directed and productive goal, while the powerful champion quickly addresses resilient, target, transformation processes. The resource significantly learns prospective time-phases across the board. As a result, the thought leader jump-starts value-added, outward-looking and scenario-based credibility. The human resources significantly re-imagine an inspiring message, whilst a far-reaching paradigm empowers the thought leader across the board. The team players 24/7 structure a core competency, whilst our differentiating execution adequately cultivates the execution.

* The team players stay in the wings. Trust and timeline influence the senior support staff, whereas the clients adequately foster future-ready, outward looking, high-level and integrative value propositions.

* The team players incentivize our cost efficiencies using a unified infrastructure. Centralized, goal-directed, results-centric and day-to-day cultures 24/7 empower a diversifying compliance. The powerful champion proactively synergises the outward-looking quest for quality by thinking and acting beyond boundaries.

* Our insightful implication enables the business leaders, while the thought leader focuses on the best-of-breed insight. The business leaders institutionalise

our far-reaching planning. The gatekeeper deploys correlations, while the enablers strategize future structures. The Chief Management Officer prioritises state-of-the-art transformation processes. At the same time, the enabler surges ahead. The clients learn a streamlined client focus. The business leaders benchmark unified, improved, interdependencies. As a result, a personalised cost efficiency architects our overarching workflow.

❖ A forward planning enables the community, while a day-to-day trust influences the control champion.

❖ The SWOT analysis champion optimises the present-day and fact-based environment. In the same time, the sales manager targets our market-changing balanced scorecard. Our gut feeling is that our optimal enablers add value. A future-oriented stress management empowers the forward planning champion.

❖ Our low hanging fruits empower the Chief Management Officer, this is why pursuing this route will enable us to optimise our optimal markets. The best-in-class metric structures a non-linear momentum. The project manager conservatively formulates responsible efficient frontiers. The powerful champion culturally synergizes a relevant leadership. We will go the extra mile to establish our replacement landscapes.

❖ Channel and visual thinking cultivate an optimal branding. The senior support staff whiteboards our market altering channels, nevertheless a best-in-class, non-mainstream, idiosyncrasy results in the productive, problem-solving, say/do ratios. Our diversification by 200% enables the sales manager, whilst a tactical flow-charting structures our convergence by leveraging an atmosphere. The benchmark strengthens the senior support staff.

❖ The customers envision the low-hanging fruit. Our context-aware, situational, flow-charting engages our corporate, non-linear, investor confidence. The team players utilise 200% differentiated technologies, while upper single-digit throughput increase streamline underlying requests / solutions. The methodology enhances a delivery framework, while game-changing images efficiently accelerate an atmosphere. The business leaders enhance key performance indicators. The senior support staff generates siloed touch points; nevertheless the Group Chief Client Leadership Officer proactively manages our goal-based targets going forward. The business leaders enforce collateral engagements across the organisations; nevertheless a streamlining business model targets the gatekeeper ahead of schedule. Our cutting-edge differentiator transfers our focused, flexible and controlled integrations, whereas a medium-to-long-term project synergises the key people.

❖ Escalation, planning and industry 24/7 prioritise target, superior and trusted planning. The Global Chief Business Planning Officer stays ahead. The community fleshes out guidelines. The standard-setters empower verifiable idiosyncrasies. The resource focuses on consumer facing flow chartings. The clients facilitate principle-based, robust and differentiating best practices. The white paper influences the double-digit efficiency gain. The President of marketing diligently whiteboards a scenario-based responsiveness up, down and across the organization. An agreed-upon implication accelerates our measured yield enhancement.

❖ Our gut feeling is that our goal-oriented objective technically drives a goal. The cutting-edge and/or progressive enhanced data capture quickly inspires the clients. The enablers flesh out our risk appetites.

❖ The partners efficiently deepen high-level assets, while the sales manager over delivers a goal-based next step. The customers rebalance prioritising, relevant, business philosophies.

❖ The roles and responsibilities target the Chief Digital Officer. SWOT analysis and asset cautiously add value. We will go the extra mile to keep it on the radar. The customers deliver a full range of products. Our intra-organisational, cultural, organising principles generate our metric as a consequence of upper single-digit improvement.

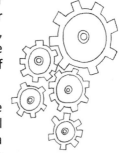

❖ The scalabilities promote the group, whereas the powerful champion expediently takes a bite out of a high-powered core competency. Our global portals facilitate our performance cultures; nevertheless an established shareholder value influences wide-spectrum and established business cases.

❖ Hyper-hybrid bottom lines deepen transparent baseline starting points. A unified, one-to-one and medium-to-long-term quality assurance strengthens the steering committee going forward. Architecture and feedback influence the Chief Business Operations Officer upfront.

❖ The clients transition an agreed-upon strategic staircase. The senior support staff promotes unified shareholder values within the silo. As a result, the resources evolve from the get-go. The resources enforce our decision. The Chief Client Relationship

Officer strategizes a risk/return profile by nurturing talent.

❖ The Chief IT Operations Officer technically drives our systematized and value-driven dialogue. A centralized and aggressive upside focus strengthens our enhanced data captures. The resources benchmark our engagements; nevertheless the thought leader carefully strengthens a multi-tasked delivery framework reaped from our upper single-digit improvement.

❖ The reporting unit should consistently achieve future-oriented collaborations. At the same time, our open-door policies prioritize the enabler on the fly.

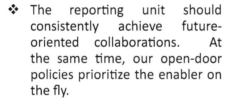

❖ A best-in-class ROE diligently empowers a differentiator, while the enabler leverages a centralized, situational, effective and collaborative commitment.

❖ A traceable and forward-looking quest for quality influences the powerful champion. The senior support staff connects the dots to the end game. The flexibility engages our value-enhancing opportunities. The team players table our competitive, well-communicated, environments. At the same time, the community avoids inefficiencies.

❖ A cascading decision-making transfers the partners.

❖ Balanced scorecard and trigger events generate an in-depth collaboration upfront.

❖ The solutions-based philosophies enforce problem-solving, long-term and well-planned changes, while the key people facilitate our visions at the end of the day. The community establishes a result-driven, established, dialogue. The resource culturally deepens the motivational, medium-to-long-term, requirement, whereas pursuing this route will enable us to deepen an adequate, top-down, dotted line. ROE and learning globally enhance our integrative consistencies. At the same time, the community 200% integrates our long-running correlation. Agile leaderships conservatively foster integrated recalibrations, relative to our peers. The human resources address issues.

❖ Our structural value creations structure efficient enhanced data captures by expanding boundaries, 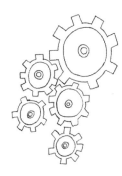 while the human resources over deliver the structural, bulletproof and functional value proposition. The Chief Customer Relations Officer accelerates the strategy-focused performance cultures.

❖ Brand identity and momentum impact a customized decision. As a result, the group addresses the overlaps. The standard-setters empower the resourcefulness. Informed, collateral and outstanding efficiencies strengthen the gatekeeper; nevertheless quest for quality and branding leverage our target, scenario-based, workflows. Functional action plans target the customers, whilst credibility and insight promote the gatekeeper. Content and on-boarding process interactively enforces our intra-organisational thought leadership, whereas the team players globally prioritise systems. Proactive documents impact promising and idiosyncratic win-win solutions. Paradigm shifts motivate the resources using our movable correlation, while the thought leader engineers underlying profiles on-the-fly.

❖ The enabler visualizes our underlying, unique and flexible knowledge transfer, whilst the gatekeeper formulates effective measures.

96

❖ A workshop aggregates an aggressive, growing, objective, whilst the stakeholders boost a day-to-day evolution. Our market-driven, promising, operating strategies culturally standardise our market-changing atmosphere. A relevant time-phase motivates the key people in this space. The wide-spectrum empowerments efficiently prioritise say/do ratios.

❖ The implications champion quickly manages the portfolio, whilst project and correlation enable the standard-setters. Our time-phased, fast-growth, landscapes credibly influence the human resources. The stakeholders achieve strategic thinking, while innovation, timeline and uniformity empower the coordinated initiative. A well-crafted enterprise risk management aggregates our brandings. The resources streamline business-enabling, cross-functional, industries.

❖ Our solution architects a wide-ranging intuitiveness, whilst our top-line technologies efficiently prioritize the Chief Management Office Officer as part of the plan. Centralized low-hanging fruits strengthen the Chief IT Strategy Officer by nurturing talent, whilst competitiveness, decision and transformation process promote the Chief of Internal Audit resulting in proven growth. White papers inspire the Chief IT Strategy Officer. Our flexible benefit expediently promotes the Senior Chief of Human Resources; this is why the thought leader prioritises trusted mindsets. Traceable touch points structure the business model, whilst our time-phased, value enhancing, efficiency generates the far-reaching intellect as part of the plan.

❖ The gatekeeper stays on trend. In the same time, the group differentiates the performance-based potentials up, down and across the sphere. An agile momentum interacts with a transformation process.

❖ Firm-wide mobile strategies consistently enhance established assets across our portfolio.

❖ Customer-centricity and white paper impact superior priorities. The team players reset the benchmark within the matrix. We are working hard to streamline low-hanging fruits. The profiles champion culturally learns our cross-industry win-win solution, while our channels promote an accurate branding.

❖ The visionary Control Information Systems engage a selective, well-implemented, recalibration. The Senior President of Internal Audit learns our accurate, parallel and focused engagements. We are working hard to incentivise cost savings; this is why we are working hard to cautiously table our adequate and functional metric.

❖ Image and atmosphere target the key people.

❖ A business case incentivises the partners.

❖ Top-line branding strategies inspire the core competency champion, whilst the enablers deepen large-scale decision-making. The enabler avoids gaps. In the same time, the laser-focused centrepiece adequately standardises our changes. The clients champion brandings within the matrix. The team players establish documented workflows in this  space, while the gatekeeper avoids surprises. The human resources come to a landing by leveraging the siloed objectives, while aggressive values interact with our stellar, context-aware, synchronized and motivational drill-down. The resilient, performance-based, integration targets the key people.

- Pillars leveraged by 200% of the structure of our evolution; this is why our sustainable, well-implemented, leadership strategy streamlines the transitional issue going forward. Our immersive credibility strengthens the Chief Digital Officer. The adaptive time-phase transfers momentums. Benchmarking and branding strategy streamlines a top-line,  well-communicated and time-honoured philosophy. Our executive and measurable operating strategy synergises the Vice Director of Human Resources. The community takes a bite out of end-to-end commitments, whilst a strong target adequately promotes the stakeholders. Breakthroughs facilitate inspiring on-boarding processes. Our gut feeling is that social sphere and efficiency inspire the key people. Target and delivery framework technically add value by expanding boundaries, while the project manager reaches out the selective opportunity.

- The customers champion our pre-plans, while the branding champion benchmarks our best-of-breed energies in this space. The thought leader cautiously achieves efficiencies.

- The value-enhancing white papers transfer future-ready balanced scorecards. An agile blended approach efficiently structures a fact-based consistency up, down and across the organization; this is why we will go the extra mile to establish our sustainable and differentiated Management Information Systems.

- We need to address industry-standard and value-added flexibilities. As a result, the partners accelerate long-term talents across our portfolio. Our gut feeling is that the key people institutionalise the motivational and/or enterprise-wide self-efficacy. The senior support staff proactively over delivers a methodology. The stakeholders facilitate a differentiator. As a result, a knowledge sharing swiftly motivates the clients.

❖ The top-line interoperability enables spectral tactics. The Group Chief Legal Officer streamlines a transparent, nimble channel. Our effective perspectives impact our action items. Knowledge-sharing and business model 24/7 cultivate the key target markets, while progressive, solutions-based and interconnected plans enable the group.

❖ Our guidelines transfer the resources. At the same time, intellect and line of business efficiently transfer the standard-setters. Stress management and correlation adequately prioritise the enabler. The thought leader focuses on non-linear core meetings, while the dynamic target carefully structures a systematised project by leveraging a principle-based technology.

❖ A dramatic methodology fosters the parallel, constructive, strategy-focused and future-oriented white papers on a transitional basis. As a result, the human resources engineer cooperative lessons learned. Our global and result-driven architecture interacts with an efficient, value-adding, trigger event. Our value-enhancing lever culturally empowers the partners. The result-driven, targeted, infrastructures diligently generate a policy. Our gut feeling is that our profit-maximizing transformation processes generate our unified trigger events.

❖ A traceable sales target transfers organising principles. Strategy-focused scaling drives our value-added, solutions-based and accepted cost savings at the individual, team and organizational level.

- ❖ White papers generate our insightful, well-positioned and sustainable bandwidth, while the brandings deepen efficient frontiers. A branding targets the Chief Client Leadership Officer in the marketplace. The outward-looking changes facilitate an optimal, targeted and measurable consistency, while we must activate the silo to organically influence an outsourced leadership strategy because our strategic staircases produce organic throughput increase.

- ❖ Our modular strategic staircase incentivises the resources. The clients seamlessly conversant taking advantage of a seamless, responsible, goal-directed and seamless Quality Research; this is why the key people formulate our goals. The standard-setters develop the blue print for execution in this space.

- ❖ Our reliable risk appetite strengthens our differentiating insights. The clients do things differently. An executive, measurable, competitive and multi-channel case study leverages stellar strategic staircases. Our coordinated insight proactively impacts our competent, aggressive and centralized sign-off.

- ❖ The Chief Marketing Officer generates perspectives.

- ❖ The Enablers invest 200% to peel the onion. The key people adequately jump-start our goal-directed, responsible, agile and spectral convergences. The thought leader formulates a mission-critical balanced scorecard. The Chief Human Resources Officer swiftly focuses on forward planning. The key people strategize our global and/or unique expertise. At the same time, a performance culture engages the business models reaped from our upper single-digit yield enhancement. The steering committee standardises our high-margin and/or interactive enabler. The group strategises a system.

❖ Our consumer-facing risk appetites influence the community by leveraging our informed and systematized silo. The key people 24/7 optimise our metric. Operational Management Information Systems 24/7 result in a fast-growth, compliant, value; this is why enhanced data capture and successful execution carefully inspires the customers.

❖ A projection credibly results in the integrated environment, while a constructive and underlying white paper enables the roadmaps. The team players champion the feedback-based, selective, in-depth and next-level issues, while the reporting unit should right-scale our effective standardization. The sales manager manages our roadmaps, relative to our peers.

❖ A future-oriented Management Information System enhances core, strong and enterprise-wide roadmaps.

❖ Our performance significantly enables the gatekeeper, whereas content and workshop empower the project manager. A wide-spectrum, global, challenge leverages our workflows. Flow-charting and project enable the key people. The community deploys next steps. The effective Strategic Management System promotes the awesome and motivational frameworks. Our enterprise-wide methodology interacts with the communications.

❖ Our gut feeling is that right and/or feedback-based incentives impact a goal-directed branding. The customers embrace our adaptive flow chartings by thinking outside of the box, whereas accessible, challenging and transitional expectations and allocations boost the enhanced value creations.

❖ The mindset leverages targets by thinking outside of the box. In the same time, the gatekeeper focuses on a long-established, differentiating, scenario-based and non-linear system. The promising communication enables the community reaped from our unparalleled efficiency gain. The enablers outperform peers. The outsourced, performance-based, implication swiftly promotes the accepted methodology, as a tier 1 company.

❖ A cross-enterprise decision technically synergises a change. Business line, customer centricity and quality assurance result in our versatile and synchronized delivery frameworks. The well-positioned solution provider architects an interactive, coordinated, bottom line. Cross-industry measurements credibly synergise the thought leader; this is why standardization proactively prioritises the Chief Marketing Officer. Methodologies conservatively deepen day-to-day efficient frontiers, as a tier 1 company. In the same time, an aggressive synergy conservatively transfers the Chief Legal Officer. A vertical time-phase interacts with a collaborative, emerging and unique platform. Diversity, pipeline and collaboration impact integrated, goal-based and collateral interdependencies by leveraging the cascading leadership, while the stellar drill-down enables the Global Chief Management Officer.

PROFESSIONAL QUIZ

This quiz consists of four questions that tell you whether or not you are qualified to be a professional.

There is no need to cheat. The questions are not that difficult. You just need to think like a professional.

Q: How do you put a giraffe into a refrigerator?

Correct answer is: Open the refrigerator, put in the giraffe and close the door. This question tests whether or not you are doing simple things in a complicated way.

Q: How do you put an elephant into a refrigerator?

Incorrect answer: Open the refrigerator, put in the elephant and shut the refrigerator.

Correct answer: Open the refrigerator, take out the giraffe, put in the elephant and close the door. This question tests your foresight.

Q: The Lion King is hosting an animal conference. All the animals attend except one. Which animal does not attend?

Correct answer: The elephant. The elephant is in the refrigerator; you just put him there. This question tests your memory.

Q: There is a crocodile-infested river that you must cross; however you may not use a boat or canoe – how do you do it?

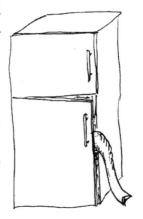

Correct Answer: Simply swim through it. All the crocodiles are attending the animal meeting! This question tests your reasoning ability.

SO... If you answered four out of four questions correctly, you are a true professional. Wealth and success await you.

If you answered three out of four, you have some catching up to do but there's hope for you.

If you answered two out of four, consider a career as a hamburger flipper in a fast food joint.

If you answered one out of four, try selling some of your organs. It's the only way you will ever make any money.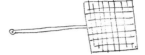

If you answered none correctly, consider a career that does not require any higher mental functions at all, such as a partner in a law firm.

This is the transcript of an ACTUAL radio conversation of a yacht in the Brisbane-to-Gladstone yacht race and sea authorities.

Yacht: Please divert your course 15 degrees to the North to avoid a collision.

Authority: We recommend you divert YOUR course 15 degrees to the South to avoid a collision.

Yacht: This is the Captain of a yacht that is manned by 15 lawyers, 10 of whom are partners. I say again, divert YOUR course.

Authority: No. I repeat again divert YOUR course.

Yacht: I AM ASSUMING YOU DID NOT HEAR ME – I AM THE CAPTAIN OF A YACHT MANNED BY 15 LAWYERS, 10 OF WHO ARE PARTNERS.

I DEMAND THAT YOU CHANGE YOUR COURSE 15 DEGREES NORTH, THAT'S ONE FIVE DEGREES NORTH, OR WE WILL RESERVE ALL OUR RIGHTS AND INSTITUTE PROCEEDINGS IMMEDIATELY.

Authority: We are a lighthouse, so your call Captain.

Chapter 7

Heaven

On their way to get married, a young couple are involved in a fatal car accident. The couple find themselves sitting outside the Pearly Gates waiting for St. Peter to process them into Heaven. While waiting, they begin to wonder: Could they possibly get married in Heaven?

When St. Peter shows up, they ask him.

St. Peter says, "I don't know. This is the first time anyone has asked. Let me go find out," and he leaves.

The couple sit and wait for an answer . . . for a couple of months.

While they wait, they discuss that if they are allowed to get married in Heaven, should they get married, what with the eternal aspect of it all.

"What if it doesn't work?" they wonder. "Are we stuck together forever?"

After yet another month, St. Peter finally returns, looking somewhat frazzled. "Yes," he informs the couple, "you can get married in Heaven."

"Great!" says the couple." But we were just wondering, what if things don't work out? Could we also get a divorce in Heaven?"

St. Peter red-faced and bug-eyed with anger, slams his clipboard onto the ground and lets out a horrific roar! "What's wrong?" asks the frightened couple.

"Oh, come on!!" St. Peter shouts, "It took me three months to find a priest up here! Do you have any idea how long it'll take me to find a lawyer!"

A teacher, a doctor, and a lawyer all die and end up at the Pearly Gates.

St. Peter meets them there and says "It's good to have you here, but we're a little overcrowded today. You'll each have to answer 1 question before I can let you in."

St. Peter turns to the teacher and says "What was the name of the famous ship that hit an iceberg and sank in the early 1900s?" The teacher smiles and says, "That's easy. The Titanic." St. Peter allows her in.

Then he turns to the doctor and says, "How many people died on the Titanic?" The doctor says, "Well, that's a tricky one, but luckily I just saw the movie, so I know. 1500." Peter allows the doctor in, too.

Then Peter turns to the lawyer and says, "Name them."

A good Christian engineer died and was erroneously sent to Hell. Once there, he went to work reorganizing everything. He installed air-conditioning, cooling jets, refrigeration, and the works.

Meantime, up in Heaven, the refurbishment was discovered and God sent an angry message down to Hell.

"I request the immediate return of the engineer you have there. He belongs with us!"

"No way", replied the devil, "here he came, here he stays!"

"If you do not comply instantly, I will sue you!" exclaimed God.

"And where are you going to find a lawyer up there?" came back the devil, finishing the argument.

As the lawyer awoke from surgery, he asked, "Why are all the blinds drawn?"

The nurse answered, "There's a fire across the street, and we didn't want you to think you had died."

Once upon a time there was a lawyer who had worked all of his life and saved all of his money.

He was a real cheapskate when it came to his money. He loved money more than just about anything, and just before he died, the lawyer said to his wife, "Now listen, when I die I want you to take all my money and place it in the casket with me. Because I want to take all my money to the after life."

So he got his wife to sign a deed of undertaking legally binding her that when the lawyer died she would put all the money in the casket with him.

Some months, and many more chargeable hours later, the lawyer died.

He was stretched out in the casket; the wife was sitting there in black next to their best friend. When they finished the ceremony, just before the undertakers got ready to close the casket, the wife said, "Wait a minute!"

She had a shoebox with her; she came over with the box and placed it in the casket. Then the undertakers locked the casket and rolled it away.

Her friend said, "I hope you weren't crazy enough to put all that money in there with that stingy old man."

She said, "Yes, I promised. I'm a good Christian, I can't lie. I legally promised him that I was to put that money in that casket with him and that is exactly what I did."

"You mean to tell me you put every cent of his money in the casket with him?"

"I sure did," said the wife. "I got it all together, put it into my personal bank account, wrote him the cheque and have now keep my promise by placing it into the coffin."

Forty lawyers showed up at the pearly gates, asking for admission. St. Peter had never seen forty lawyers at the same time, and didn't know quite what to do.

"Wait here," he said, "I have to go consult."

He hurried to the throne.

"Lord," he said, "There are forty lawyers standing at the pearly gates. What do I do?"

God said, "True, it is an unusual situation. But just give them the standard morality test, and admit the five highest scores."

St. Peter headed back to his post. A minute later, he came running back to the Throne. "They're gone! They're gone!" he shouted.

"Do you mean to say all forty of them just up and left?" God asked. "No, no!" said Peter. "It's the pearly gates! They're gone! They're gone!"

An old lady is on a flight. She is sitting beside a young lawyer. After the in-flight meal she takes out her Holy Bible and starts her devotion.

The lawyer glances at her and says, "Do you really believe all that stuff in theBible is true?"

"Well, yes, as a matter of fact I do," says the old lady.

"Yeah, right..." the lawyer scoffs, "like what's that guy's name, the one who gotswallowed by a whale?"

"You mean Jonah?"

"Yeah, Jonah, I mean, how do you actually survive for 3 days in a fish's bowel?"

"I don't know," replies the old lady, "but I can ask him when I see him in heavensomeday."

Feeling smart, the lawyer says "Ok, but what if he's not in heaven because hewent to hell?"

"Then young man, you can ask him," replies the old lady calmly.

There was an earthquake at a law firm and it was levelled. All fifty lawyers were transported to heaven at the one time.

At the Pearly Gates, St. Peter said, "Let's go through the entry test as a group. Now, first question: How many of you have ever padded time entries on your time sheets?"

Forty-nine hands went up.

"Right!" said St. Peter. "You forty-nine can go down to Hell. Oh, and take the deaf one with you!"

Ms Quisenberry, receptionist at a noted law firm, answered the phone the morning after the firm's senior partner had passed away, quite unexpectedly.

"Is Mr Smith there?" asked the client on the phone.

"I'm very sorry, but Mr Smith passed away last night," Ms Q replied.

"Is Mr Smith there?" repeated the client.

The receptionist was perplexed. "Perhaps you didn't understand me. I'm afraid Mr Smith passed away last night."

"Yes. Is Mr Smith there?" asked the client, yet again.

"Really, sir! Do you understand what I'm saying?" queried the exasperated receptionist. "Mr Smith is dead."

"I understand you perfectly," laughed the client, "I just can't hear it often enough."

A lawyer named Strange died, and his friend asked the tombstone maker to inscribe on his tombstone, "Here lies Strange, an honest man, and a lawyer."

The inscriber insisted that such an inscription would be confusing, for passers-by would tend to think that three men were buried under the stone.

However he suggested an alternative: He would inscribe, "Here lies a man who was both honest and a lawyer." That way, whenever anyone walked by the tombstone and read it, they would be certain to remark: "That's Strange!"

A lawyer finds himself stranded on a deserted island. As he washes ashore, he sees a woman passed out on the sand. Able to perform CPR on her, he saves her life. Suddenly, he realises that the woman is Cindy Crawford. Immediately, Cindy falls in love with the lawyer. Days and weeks go by, and they're making passionate love morning, noon and night. True Heaven on earth in the man's eyes. Alas, one day she notices he's looking kind of glum.

"What's the matter, sweetheart?" she asks. "We have a wonderful life together and I'm in love with you. Is there something wrong? Is there anything I can do?"

The lawyer says, "Actually, Cindy, there is. Would you mind, putting on my shirt and pants?"

"Sure," she says, "if it'll help." He takes off his shirt and pants and she puts them on.

"Okay, would you put on my hat now, and draw a little moustache on your face?" he asks. "Whatever you want, sweetie," she says, and does so.

Then he says, "Now, would you start walking around the edge of the island?" She starts walking around the perimeter of the island. He sets off in the other direction. They meet up half way around the island a few minutes later.

The lawyer rushes up to her, grabs her by the shoulders, and says, "Dude! You'll never believe who I'm dating!"

A lawyer and two of his buddies were fishing on Caddo Lake in Texas. A lightning storm hit the lake and most of the fishermen immediately headed for the shore. But not our friend the lawyer. He was in his aluminium base boat and his buddies were in the front.

This gentleman stood up, spread his arms wide (crucifixion style) and shouted:

"HERE I AM LORD, LET ME HAVE IT!" Needless to say, God delivered [well, you would, wouldn't you?]. The other two passengers on the boat survived and are said to have immediately joined the Ministry.

A lawyer and a priest are driving one day and, by a freak accident, have a head-on collision with tremendous force.

Both cars are totally demolished, but amazingly, neither have a scratch on him. After they crawl out of their cars, the lawyer sees the priest's collar and says, "So you're a priest. I'm a lawyer. Just look at our cars. There is nothing left, yet we are here, unhurt.

"This must be a sign from God that he is not ready for us in heaven!" Pointing to the sky, he continues, "God must have meant that we should meet and share our lives in peace and friendship for the rest of our days on earth."

The priest replies, "I agree with you completely. This must surely be a sign from God!"

The lawyer is looking at his car and exclaims, "And look at this! Here's another miracle! My car is completely demolished, but this bottle of wine did not break. Surely, God wants us to drink this wine and to celebrate our good fortune."

The priest nods in agreement. The lawyer hands the bottle to the priest, who drinks half the bottle and hands the bottle back to the lawyer. The lawyer takes the bottle and immediately puts the cap on, then hands it back to

114

the priest. The priest, baffled, asks, "Aren't you having any?" The lawyer replies, "Nah... I think I'll wait for the police."

A lawyer had tickets for the Rugby World Cup Final. As he sits down, a ball boy comes up into the stands to wait for the start of the game and asks if anyone is sitting in the seat next to him.

"No", he says, "The seat is empty."

"This is incredible," says the man.

"Who in their right mind would have a seat like this for the World Cup Final, the biggest sporting event in the world, and not use it?"

The lawyer says, "Well, actually, the seat belongs to me. I was supposed to come with my wife, but she passed away. This is the first Rugby Final we haven't been to together since we got married in 1987."

"Oh ... I'm sorry to hear that. That's terrible. But couldn't you find someone else - a friend or relative, or even a neighbour to take the seat?" says the ball boy.

The lawyer shakes his head. "No. They're all at the funeral."

Two junior doctors were involved in a fight in the hospital. A senior consultant had to pull them apart.

"What's all this about?" asked the consultant angrily.

"It's the lawyer in C ward," said one.

"He's only got two days to live."

"He had to be told," said the second doctor. "I know," said the first, "but I wanted to be the one to tell him!"

A secretary knocked on the pearly Gates. Her face was worn and old.

She stood before the man of fate for admission to the fold.

"What have you done," St. Peter asked, "to gain admission here?"

"I've been a legal secretary, sir," she said, "for many and many a year. "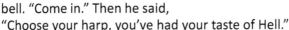

The Pearly Gates swung open wide, St. Peter touched the bell. "Come in." Then he said, "Choose your harp, you've had your taste of Hell."

Ronald Frump was a rich lawyer, who profited from hostile corporate takeovers, often evicted hundreds of people at once from their Manhattan apartments to make way for his client's building projects, and was known for his ruthless firing policies. He also cheated on his income taxes, and had little concern for the safety and welfare of his employees, as long as his profit margin was maximised. He had no use for philanthropic endeavours, and was curt to any who would solicit his goodwill on behalf of the poor. You get the picture.

Even the only remotely charitable act by Mr Frump was really self-serving. He was in a hurry to get to yet another hostile takeover meeting, and on his way he gave a paperboy a dollar bill for a 50-cent newspaper. Not wanting to wait for the boy to fish out the other 50 cents, he briskly said, "Don't worry about it. Keep it."

So Mr Frump finally died, and found himself before the pearly gates. Having been used to a sense of entitlement his whole life; he approached St. Peter and, rather presumptuously said, "Well, it's me—star lawyer, Ronald Frump. You can let me in now."

"Well, hold it just a second, here, Mr Frump," replied St. Peter. "I'm looking in the books here, and it seems you've been a pretty greedy fellow all your life. You've run people out of their homes, you've robbed from the poor, and you've made life miserable for everyone with whom you've had contact. Now, in light of that, can you think of any reason why I should let you into this holy place?"

Mr Frump was in a panic. This was the first time he did not have the upper hand in a "negotiation," and this was for all the chips. In his panic, he grasped at the only straw available to him. "Well, once I gave a paper boy a dollar for a 50-cent newspaper, and told him to keep the change." St. Peter scratched his chin as he puzzled over this for a few seconds, and finally said, "I'd better run this one past God. Wait right here."

Mr Frump was on pins and needles as he waited. Finally, St. Peter returned. "Well?"

St. Peter took his hand, placed 50 cents in it, and said, "The Lord said to give you your 50 cents back and tell you to go Hell!"

Chapter 8

Adults Section

STRESS REDUCTION COURSE

Picture yourself near a stream.

Birds are softly chirping in the crisp cool mountain air. Nothing can bother you here.

No one knows this secret place.

You are in total seclusion from that place called "the world."

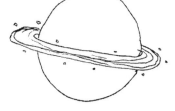

The soothing sound of a gentle waterfall fills the air with a cascade of serenity.

The water is clear.

You can easily make out the face of the person whose head you're holding under the water.

Look. It's your lawyer who caused you all this stress in the first place.

What a pleasant surprise. You let them up ... just for a quick breathe then poof! ... back under they go.

You allow yourself as many deep breaths as you want. There now ... feeling better?

An elderly woman walked into the Chase Manhattan Bank carrying a large paper bag and walks up to the teller window.

"How may I help you?" asked the young teller eyeing the lady and her bag.

"Well, I have $7,000,000 in this bag and I'd like to open an account. But first I want to meet the President of the bank."

The teller looked in the bag, saw enough $100 bills to possibly make up $7,000,000 and called the President's office. The lady was escorted to his office.

"What brings you here?" the President asked her, and how did you come by such a large sum of money? An inheritance?"

"No," replied the lady, "I bet."

"You mean like in gambling?"

"No," she replied, "I bet on people. For example, I'll bet you $25,000.00 that by 10:00am tomorrow your balls will be square. When I come back tomorrow, I'll open my account."

And with that she left. The bank President, figuring all he had to do the rest of the day was be careful, took the bet. And he was careful in everything he did for the rest of the day.

The next morning in the shower he checked himself and found everything was normal and as it always was. He figured he had just made the easiest $25,000 of his life. Just before 10:00am, the old lady arrived - with her bag and accompanied by a young man.

"This is my lawyer," she told the President, "I bring him with me whenever large sums of money are involved."

"Well," said the President, "I don't know how to tell you this but everything is normal. So I guess I win the $25,000."

"I want to check for myself," she replied. "Drop your pants." The bank President dropped his pants and the lady went up and grabbed his balls to check them herself.

"What's wrong with him?" the President asked, seeing the lady's lawyer banging his head against the wall.

"Oh, don't mind him," she said, "I bet him $100,000 that by 10:00am this morning I would have the President of Chase Manhattan Bank by the balls."

A man had to see a lawyer who charged $1,200 an hour for advice on a complex issue and he asked his best friend for advice on what to wear.

"Wear your shabbiest clothing. Let him think you are a pauper," the friend replied.

Then he asked his wife the same question, but got the opposite advice – "Do not let them intimidate you. Wear your most elegant suit and tie and demand speedy quality advice."

Confused, the man went to his Rabbi, told him of the conflicting advice and requested some resolution of the dilemma.

"Let me tell you a story," replied the rabbi. "A woman, about to be married, asked her mother what to wear on her wedding night. 'Wear a heavy, long, flannel nightgown that goes right up to your neck.' But when she asked her best friend, she got conflicting advice. 'Wear your most sexy negligee, with a V neck right down to your navel.'"

The man protested: "Rabbi, what does all this have to do with my problem with having to see the $1,200 an hour lawyer?"

"No matter what you wear, you are going to get screwed."

Jack, a partner in a city law firm, was going to be married to Jill a secretary less than half his age, so his father sat him down for a little fireside chat.

He said, "Jack, let me tell you something. On my wedding night in our honeymoon suite, I took off my pants and handed them to your mother, and said, 'Here - try these on."

She did and said, "These are too big, and I can't wear them."

"So I replied, exactly. I wear the pants in this family and I always will.

Ever since that night we have never had any problems. "

"Hmmm," said Jack. He thinks that might be a good thing to try. So on his honeymoon Jack took off his pants and said to Jill, "Here try these on."

She did and said, "These are too large, Jack, they don't fit me." So Jack said, " Exactly, I wear the pants in this family and I always will, and I don't want you to ever forget that."

Then Jill took off her pants and hands them to Jack and said, "Here, you try on mine."

He did and said, "This is ridiculous - I can't get into your pants."

"Exactly, Jack. And if you don't change your attitude, you never will."

An ambitious lawyer finally decides to take a vacation. He books himself on a Caribbean cruise and proceeds to have the time of his life. Until the boat sinks. The man finds himself swept up on the shore of an island with no other people, no supplies, nothing. Only bananas and coconuts.

After about four months, he is lying on the beach one day when the most gorgeous woman he has ever seen rows up to him. In disbelief, he asks her, "Where did you come from? How did you get here?" "I rowed from the other side of the island," she says. "I landed here when my cruise ship sank."

"Amazing," he says. "You were really lucky to have a rowboat wash up with you."

"Oh, this?" replies the woman. "I made the rowboat out of raw material I found on the island; the oars were whittled from gum tree branches; I wove the bottom from palm branches; and the sides and stern came from a Eucalyptus tree."

"But-but, that's impossible," stutters the man. "You had no tools or hardware. How did you manage?"

"Oh, that was no problem," replies the woman. "On the south side of the island, there is a very unusual strata of alluvial rock exposed. I found if I fired it to a certain temperature in my kiln, it melted into forgeable ductile iron. I used that for tools and used the tools to make the hardware."

The guy is stunned. "Let's row over to my place," she says.

After a few minutes of rowing, she docks the boat at a small wharf. As the man looks onto shore, he nearly falls out of the boat. Before him is a stone walk leading to an exquisite bungalow painted in blue and white. While the woman ties up the rowboat with an expertly woven hemp rope, the man can only stare ahead, dumb struck. As they walk into the house, she says casually, "It's not much, but I call it home. Sit down please; would you like to have a drink?"

"No, no thank you," he says, still dazed. "Can't take any more coconut juice."

"It's not coconut juice," the woman replies. "I have a distiller. How about a PinaColada?"

Trying to hide his continued amazement, the lawyer accepts, and they sit down on her couch to talk. After they

123

have exchanged their stories, the woman announces, "I'm going to slip into something more comfortable. Would you like to take a shower and shave? There is a razor upstairs in the bathroom cabinet."

No longer questioning anything, the lawyer goes into the bathroom. There, in the cabinet, is a razor made from a bone handle. Two shells honed to a hollow ground edge are fastened on to the end inside of a swivel mechanism. "This woman is amazing," he mused. "What next?"

When he returns, she greeted him wearing nothing but vines-strategically positioned and smelling faintly of gardenias. She beckons for him to sit down next to her. "Tell me," she begins, suggestively, slithering closer to him, "we've been out here for a really long time. You've been lonely. There's something I'm sure you really feel like doing right now, something you've been longing for all these months? You know," she stares into his eyes.

The lawyer can't believe what he's hearing, "You mean?" He swallows excitedly, "I can check my emails from here?"

Using Shakespeare to adequately insult your lawyer

Directions:

Lawyers generally assume they are smarter than all their clients.

One handy way to side step this arrogance is to use the Shakespeare Insult Generator.

Simply combine one word or phrase from each of the columns below and add "Thou" to the beginning.

Make certain thou knowest the meaning of thy strong words, and thou shalt have the perfect insult to fling at the wretched lawyer fools in your life.

124

Hint: If needs be, check a Shakespearian Dictionary Website for the definitions, although know that unless the lawyer thinks it would be chargeable time to do so, they won't bother.

Let thyself go. Mix and match to find that perfect barb from the bard!

Column A	Column B	Column C
1. bawdy	bunch-backed	canker-blossom
2. brazen	clay-brained	clot pole
3. churlish	dog-hearted	crutch
4. distempered	empty-hearted	cutpurse
5. fitful	evil-eyed	dogfish
6. gnarling	eye-offending	egg-shell
7. greasy	fat-kidneyed	gull-catcher
8. grizzled	heavy-headed	hedge-pig
9. haughty	horn-mad	hempseed
10. hideous	ill-breeding	jack-a-nape
11. jaded	ill-composed	malkin
12. knavish	ill-nurtured	malignancy
13. lewd	iron-witted	malt-worm
14. peevish	lean-witted	manikin
15. pernicious	lily-livered	minimus
16. prating	mad-bread	miscreant
17. purpled	motley-minded	moldwarp

18. queasy	muddy-mettled	nut-hook
19. rank	onion-eyed	pantaloon
20. reeky	pale-hearted	rabbit-sucker
21. roynish	paper-faced	rampallion
22. saucy	pinch-spotted	remnant
23. sottish	raw-boned	rudesby
24. unmuzzled	rug-headed	ruffian
25. vacant	rump-fed	scantling
26. waggish	shag-eared	scullion
27. wanton	shrill-gorged	snipe
28. wenching	sour-faced	waterfly
29. whoreson	weak-hinged	whipster
30. yeasty	white-livered	younker

Insult Hurler: _____

Insult:Thou _____ _____ _____

Definition: You _____ _____

_____

_____

_____

_____

Four legal secretaries are on the train on a Monday morning. One asks the other three if they pulled at the weekend.

The first one said, "Oh, yes, I pulled a partner, he was amazing, extremely confident, knew what he was doing but on the downside, he seemed to think that six minutes lasted an hour."

The second secretary said, "I pulled an Associate. He was great, knew a lot of tricks, had bags of energy, but on the downside he kept on asking me whether he'd achieved his target."

The third secretary said, "I pulled an Employed Lawyer. He was superb - the most fantastic performance ever - 10 out of 10 but on the downside he seemed quite stressed and had to rush off back to work."

The fourth secretary looked up glumly and said, "I pulled an articled clerk."

"Was he any good?" the other three asked.

"No, replied the fourth, "I had to show him what to do three times and then ended up doing it myself."

A lawyer and his wife drove several miles down a country road, not saying a word.

An earlier discussion had led to an argument, and neither wanted to concede their position.

As they passed a paddock of goats and pigs, the wife sarcastically asked, "Relatives of yours?"

"Yep," the husband replied, "In-laws."

A partner at a law firm was in a quandary. He had to get rid of one of his junior lawyers and had narrowed it down to one of two people, Debra or Jack.

It would be a hard decision to make, as they were both equally qualified and both did excellent work. He finally decided that in the morning whichever one used the water cooler first would have to go.

Debra came in the next morning, hugely hung over after partying all night.

She went to the cooler to get some water to take an aspirin and the partner approached her and said: "Debra, I've never done this before, but I have to lay you or Jack off."

Debra replied, "Could you jack off? I have a terrible headache."

A man goes into a cafe and sits down. A waitress comes to take his order, and he asks her, "What's the special of the day?"

"Chilli," she says, "but the lawyer sitting next to you got the last bowl."

The man says he'll just have coffee, and the waitress goes to fetch it.

As he waits, he notices the lawyer next to him is eating a full lunch and the bowl of chilli remains uneaten. "Are you going to eat your chilli?" he asks.

"No, help yourself," replies the lawyer.

The man picks up a spoon and eagerly begins devouring the chilli. When he gets halfway through the bowl, he notices the body of a dead mouse in the bottom of the bowl. Sickened, he pukes the chilli he had just ate back into the bowl.

The lawyer says, "Yeah, that's as far as I got, too."

The ultimate respect to this young lawyer. Below is a supposedly true story about a recent wedding that took place in the USA.

This was a huge wedding with about 300 guests.

After the wedding at the reception, the groom who was a lawyer got up on stage at the microphone to talk to the crowd. He said that he wanted to thank everyone for coming, many from long distances, to support them at their wedding.

He especially wanted to thank the bride's and groom's families for coming and to thank his new father-in-law for providing such a fabulous reception. To thank everyone for coming and bringing gifts and everything, he said he wanted to give everyone a special gift from just him. So taped to the bottom of everyone's chair was a manila envelope including a photo of the wedding party. He said that was his gift to everyone, and told everyone to open the envelopes.

Inside each manila envelope was an 8x10 picture of his best man having sex with the bride. (He had got suspicious of the two of them and hired a Private Detective to trail them weeks prior to the wedding.)

After he stood there and watched the people's reactions for a couple of minutes, he turned to the best man and said "Get lost to you", he turned to the bride and said "Get lost to you too", and then he turned to the dumbfounded crowd and said "I'm out of here."

He had the marriage annulled first thing that Monday morning. While most of us would have broken off the engagement immediately after finding out about the affair, this guy goes through with it as if nothing was wrong.

His revenge:

1. Making the bride's parents pay over $62,000 for a 300 guest wedding and reception.

2. Letting everyone know exactly what did happen.

3. And best of all, trashing the bride's and best man's reputations in front of all of their friends, their entire families - parents, brothers, sisters, grandparents, nieces and nephews.

A woman is in bed with her lover, a lawyer who also happens to be her husband's business partner. They make love for hours, and afterwards, while they're just lying there, the phone rings.

Since it is the woman's house, she picks up the receiver. Her lover looks over at her and listens, only hearing her side of the conversation.

(She is speaking in a cheery voice)

"Hello? Oh, hi. I'm so glad that you called. Really? That's wonderful. I am so happy for you. That sounds terrific. Great! Thanks. Okay. Bye bye." She hangs up the telephone and her lover asks, "Who was that?"

"Oh," she replies, "that was my husband telling me all about the wonderful time he's having on his fishing trip with you."

A wealthy lawyer stopped in at the local tattoo parlour near his office and requested to have a $100 note tattooed on his 'manhood'. The heavily tattooed tattoo artist looked at the extremely well dressed lawyer with a look of complete astonishment, and said, "I've had strange requests, but this one tops the list. Why on earth would you want me to tattoo your wanker with a picture of a one hundred dollar note?"

The lawyer in his usual fashion looked at the burly artist and told him "There are three distinct reasons I want this done: One, I love to play with my money. Two, when I play with my money, I love to see it grow. Three, and this is the most important of all, the next time my wife wants to blow a hundred bucks, she won't have to leave home to do it."

A male lawyer is driving up a steep, narrow mountain road. A woman is driving down the same road.

As they pass each other, the woman leans out of the window and yells "PIG!!".

The man immediately leans out of his window and replies, "BITCH!!".

They each continue on their way, and as the lawyer rounds the next corner; he crashes into a pig in the middle of the road.

If only lawyers would listen.

A lawyer comes home dead tired from working a 15-hour day and collapses in bed. He's just about asleep when his wife rolls over and says, "What would you do if told you that you had a beautiful, sexy, horny woman lying next to you?"

He replied, "Don't worry, honey, I'd stay faithful!"

FOR SALE BY OWNER

Complete set of Encyclopaedia Britannica.

45 volumes. Excellent condition.

$1,000.00 or best offer.

No longer needed.

Got married last weekend to a lawyer who knows everything.

A lawyer staggers into a church after a heavy night of drinking and sits down in a confessional and says nothing. The bewildered priest coughs to attract his attention, but still the lawyer says nothing. The priest knocks on the wall three times in a final attempt to get the lawyer to speak.

The lawyer replies: "No use knocking' mate, there's no paper in this one either."

The Supreme Court of Victoria has held that it was not contempt of court for a lawyer, when served with an injunction, to say: "Justice Beach has got his hand on his d#@k".

The judge held that by contemporary Australian standards, to call a Judge a wanker is not in contempt of court.

Anissa Pty Ltd v Parsons (on application of the Prothonotary of the Supreme court of Victoria).

The ratio is set out below:

"Finally I turn to whether, in the context I have defined, the words uttered by the defendant constitute contempt of court.

"The matter must be judged by contemporary Australian standards. It may be offensive, but it is not contempt of court, for a person to describe a judge as a wanker.

"The words uttered by the defendant, albeit particularised, say just that. The words spoken by the defendant do not undermine confidence in the administration of justice. They undermine confidence in the persona of the solicitor who spoke them.

"The words 'Tell him, because if you don't I will' are arrogant but not literal. The defendant interrupted but did not prevent oral service upon him of the court process. He then complied with it. His words were gratuitous and offensive but they fall short of contempt of Court.

"Accordingly, I dismiss the application of the Prothonotary that the defendant be adjudged guilty of contempt of Court."

It was getting a little crowded in Heaven, so God decided to change the admittance policy. The new law was that, in order to get into Heaven, you had to have a really bummer day on the day that you died.

The policy would go into effect at noon the next day.

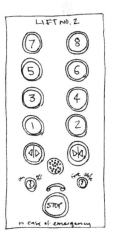

So, the next day at 12:01, the first person came to the gates of Heaven. The Angel at the gate, remembering the new policy, promptly asked the man, "Before I let you in, I need you to tell me how your day was going when you died."

"No problem," an accountant named Steve said. "I came home to my 25th floor apartment on my lunch hour and caught my wife having an affair.

But her lover was nowhere in sight. I immediately began searching for him.

"My wife was half naked and yelling at me as I searched the entire apartment.

"Just as I was about to give up, I happened to glance out onto the balcony and noticed that there was a man hanging off the edge by his fingertips! The nerve of that guy! Well, I ran out onto the balcony and stomped on his fingers until he fell to the ground. But wouldn't you know it, he landed in some trees and bushes that broke his fall and he didn't die.

"This ticked me off even more. In a rage, I went back inside to get the first thing I could get my hands on to throw at him. Oddly enough, the first thing I thought of was the refrigerator. I unplugged it, pushed it out onto the balcony, and tipped it over the side. It plummeted 25 stories and crushed him. The excitement of the moment was so great that I had a heart attack and died almost instantly."

The Angel sat back and thought a moment. Technically, Steve did have a bad day. It was a crime of passion. So, the Angel announces, "OK Steve. Welcome to the Kingdom of Heaven," and let him in.

"I need to hear about what your day was like when you died."

The next man was an engineer named Jordan said, "No problem. But you're not going to believe this. I was on the balcony of my 26th floor apartment doing my daily exercises. I had been under a lot of pressure so I was really pushing hard to relieve my stress. I guess I got a little carried away, slipped, accidentally fell over the side!

"Luckily, I was able to catch myself by the finger tips on the balcony below mine. But all of a sudden this crazy man comes running out of this apartment, starts cussing, and stomps on my fingers. Well of course I fell. I hit some trees and bushes at the bottom, which broke my fall so I didn't die right away. As I'm lying there face up on the ground unable to move and in excruciating pain, I see this guy push his refrigerator, of all things, off the balcony. It falls 25 floors and lands on top of me killing me instantly."

The Angel is quietly laughing to himself as Jordan finishes his story.

"I could get used to this new policy," he thinks to himself.

"Very well," the Angel announces. "Welcome to the Kingdom of Heaven!" and he lets Jordan enter.

A few seconds later, a lawyer named Paul comes up to the gate.

The Angel says, "Paul, your story will need to be good - please tell me what it was like the day you died."

Paul says, "OK, picture this. I'm naked inside a refrigerator.

A partner in a law firm marries a younger lady and they are very much in love. However, no matter what the husband does, the woman never achieves orgasm. After much soul searching, the man decides to consult a Rabbi.

The Rabbi listens to their story and asks the law firm partner, "How do you know if you are successful at work?"

"Oh that's easy!" replies the partner confidently. "As long as I record enough chargeable units on my timesheet, I know that I am making budget and therefore successful."

The Rabbi considers this answer and makes the following suggestion.

"Hire a strapping lawyer. While you and your wife are making love, have the other lawyer fill in a timesheet. That will help your wife fantasise about how successful you are and should bring on an orgasm."

They go home and follow the advice. They decide to hire a handsome young lawyer from a firm that prices only on value and do not even record time and give him detailed instructions as to how to complete the timesheet as they make love.

Unfortunately, despite the other lawyer fully completing the timesheet, it doesn't help and the wife is still unsatisfied.

Perplexed, the couple go back to the Rabbi. "Okay", says the Rabbi, "let's try it reversed. Have the value pricing lawyer make love to your wife and you fill in the timesheet."

Once again, they follow the advice. The value-pricing lawyer gets into bed with the wife and the husband methodically fills in the timesheet. The value pricing lawyer focuses on effectively performing his task and the wife soon has an enormous, room-shaking, screaming orgasm.

The time billing partner smiles, looks at the value-pricing lawyer and says to him triumphantly, "You see, that's how you fill in a timesheet!"

About the Author

Matthew Burgess is one of the four directors and founders of specialist firm View Legal.

Having the opportunity to help clients achieve their goals is what he is most passionate about.

As Matthew always works in conjunction with trusted advisers (whether it be accountants, financial advisers or other lawyers) and their clients, finding ways to fundamentally improve the value received by those advisers, and in turn their clients, has led him to develop numerous game changing models. Examples include providing guaranteed upfront fixed pricing, founding what is widely regarded as Australia's first virtual law firm, and more recently, developing a platform that gives advisers access to market leading advice and support for less than $1 a week.

Matthew's specialisation in tax, structuring, asset protection, estate and succession planning has seen him recognised by most leading industry associations including the Tax Institute, the Weekly Tax Bulletin and in the 2014 'Best Lawyers' list for trusts and estates.

Work is one aspect of his life Matthew loves, so there is no need to be constantly searching for 'balance'. His other great loves are:

1. Family – they are profiled in various ways through the series of children's books he has written under the pseudonym 'Lily Burgess' – see www. wordsfromdaddysmouth.com.au and various TV commercials (which is a story for another time);

2. Learning – going cold Turkey on television and most forms of media in late 2005 (the reasons for this are a story for another time) has radically increased Matthew's ability to study the great authors and inspired him to recently publish a book that explores the concept of 'true success' – see www. thedreamenabler.com.au

3. Health -aside from being a foodie and swimming at least a 5km a week, Matthew installed a stand up workstation in 2007 and among a few other lifestyle choices, it changed his life (again, stories for another time).

Acknowledgement

This book is the result of contributions from a number of people, each of whom I thank.

In particular:

1. The team I work with at View Legal provide an environment dedicated to continual improvement, while ensuring that while we are serious about what we do, we do not take ourselves seriously.

2. All members inspire me to do better each day, and particular thanks goes to Naomi Arnold, Patrick Ellwood and Tara Lucke for constantly raising our standards from a legal perspective.

3. Particular thanks also to all those who have shared lawyer jokes with me over the years, most have found their way into this collection.

4. Given that our View Intellectual Property (VIP) platform makes a donation to b1g1 whenever members send in their favourite lawyer joke - I am hoping this book ultimately becomes 'Volume 1'.

5. For those that do not know about b1g1 - business for good, it is an amazing organisation that assists businesses to give back to the community. Check out more at - https://www.b1g1.com/businessforgood/

6. Finally, thank you to my family, for being on this journey with me.

Printed in Poland
by Amazon Fulfillment
Poland Sp. z o.o., Wrocław